Abundanaire Goddess

by

Carrie Carter

Abundanaire Goddess

by Carrie Carter

ISBN: 978-1976238697

+1 – 810-334-7468

www.YourAngelChannel.com

AbundanaireGoddess@gmail.com

Angel Vision LLC

USA

➲ **Contact Carrie Carter** about keynoting, speaking, training, & spiritual consultations

Dedication

This book is dedicated to....

My husband, Jim.

Your love and inspiration is what empowered me to be an Abundanaire Goddess. You have always believed in me even when I wasn't sure I believed in myself.

You have touched the core of my soul and guide me still.

My son, Jeff.

Your strength holds me up when life throws me a curve ball. You say the right things at the right times to make me smile.

You take time out of your busy life to spend time with me. To me that's the greatest gift in the whole world. Your sense of humor and the way you look at life touches everybody that knows you. I am so proud to be able to call you my son, Jeff.

My daughter-in-law, Jenni.

You inspire me as you always look at the world in a positive way. You embrace life with a sense of adventure. I marvel at how great you are at organizing fun things to do. It may be going on a cruise, it may be going to see a concert, it may be going to a local festival. You have such a beautiful heart and you embrace life to the fullest.

My step daughter, Meg.

I am amazed at how you can juggle a family, hectic work schedule, and still find time to run off with me to play by the ocean. Your life is more balanced than you realize. You are a great wife, an amazing mother, and a great friend.

Last, but not least, I dedicate this book to my four-legged baby, Athena Marie. You have brought so much joy into my life. You and I are on a wonderful journey. You are my little angel here on earth.

The Abundanaire Goddess

by Carrie Carter

Table of Contents

The Vast Richness Of Your Life

Have you ever considered yourself to be a miracle? Truly, you are a walking, breathing, feeling, thinking, loving, living miracle. How marvelous! There may be challenges that you're dealing with (who doesn't face these?) and you may not be exactly where you'd like to be in life. But you are *here*, right now, alive. What a beautiful, extra special miracle.

Your life is rich beyond measure. You may not have a penny to your name … or you may have a bank account that rivals Paris Hilton's. You may struggle with finances, or you may be doing just fine in this arena. Perhaps you're rich in relationships, or perhaps you seek to forge stronger relationships. It may be that you find yourself rich in spirit, or it may be that you're searching for your spiritual direction. Whoever you are, and whatever your present circumstances, you've picked up this book for one simple reason—this book is for *you*.

It's for every woman who is grateful for what she has, but who knows it is her birthright to enjoy abundance in every area of her life. Yes, it *is* your birthright. God created you in love, and the energy of love is one of great abundance. You have a right to abundance with your friends and family. With your finances. With your hopes and dreams. With your creativity. With your career. With your spiritual wealth. With your joy. With love and laughter. With your wellbeing.

It begins with gratitude. First and foremost, start by acknowledging the vast richness of *your* life. There is never a need for you to feel lacking in any way. On the contrary, you are a whole person, and you already have so much! You are alive and an essential part of this grand journey of life on planet Earth, with its incredible diversity and myriad of opportunities. You are here to experience sunrises and sunsets, the calmness of a still lake, the power of crashing waves, the radiance of sunshine, the freshness of rain, the beauty of flowers, the lusciousness of ripe berries, the sound of laughter, the warmth of a hug. Are you lucky or what? What a privilege to be here, right now, to experience all that we can.

You Lucky Gal

Indeed, we're very lucky. Being a woman is a privilege, an honor, and a sheer joy. Even with PMS. Even with labor pains and stretch marks. Even with menopause. Even with all the responsibilities we carry for ourselves and others. We are spectacular and absolutely awesome! And we can be proud of our unique and very special contributions to humanity. We are endowed with wisdom, compassion, grace, endurance, strength, resolve, an intuitive awareness, and a keen sense that our spiritual side is as significant on this plane as that which we perceive with our physical senses. Indeed, we are abundantly blessed, both givers and receivers in this dance of life.

The question, then, is never one of lack. It is a matter of adaptability. How do we women, with all of our amazing strengths and our incredible power, adapt in a world that presently appears to be run by a subset of men who misuse power to control? How do we learn to achieve abundance in every aspect of our lives through cooperation, ambition, and balance, without having to resort to competition, submission, or aggression? Ladies, it can be done! You are beautifully equipped to receive tremendous abundance using your natural, God-given talents. You can do it. And you can pull others up along the way.

Cooperation, Not Competition

Cutthroat competition and aggression may get a few individuals "ahead," but at what cost? For every CEO who makes millions of dollars a year, how many entry-level workers within that same company struggle to make a living at minimum wage? For every world leader who chooses to "resolve" disputes through aggression, how many innocent civilians end up suffering? And look at what happens when a few individuals manipulate the delicate ecosystem for their own benefit (as in decimating rainforests) without regard to Mother Earth. Our environment gets out of balance and we end up with unpredictable weather. Clearly, the competitive, aggressive style of "acquiring things" is not a sustainable model. It is neither natural nor beneficial.

Your womanly trait of working in a spirit of mutual respect and cooperation yields infinitely better results. Cooperating means working with, not against, someone or something. It's a matter of recognizing that everything and everyone has a right to be, and respecting all that is around us. You are equipped with the ability to attain your own abundance without stifling, limiting, suppressing, or shortchanging yourself or others along the way. You have the means to reach your abundance while allowing all others who so choose to reach their abundance as well. Isn't this the better approach?

Rest assured, you are fully equipped to achieve riches beyond your wildest imagination. Then why, you may ask, are you not advancing as quickly as you'd like? Why does it feel like others are moving ahead, leaving you far behind? Perhaps it's a simple matter of perspective.

Millionaires can die poor, and social butterflies can die lonely. Abundance is not a matter of how much we have, or how quickly we amass it. No, it's about being fulfilled. You are living in abundance when:

- You feel that you are using your talents in a way that brings you fulfillment

- You are grateful for the resources available to you, and you use them to expand your consciousness

- The people and places you experience validate your being

- You are content with your level of giving and receiving

- You are able to express the true essence of your being

- There is ample love and positive energy both emanating from you and available for you

You are invited to continue the relationship at YourAngelChannel.com

- There is peace and calm within your soul

- You know there is great purpose to your existence

- You are able to laugh openly, with great joy

- You have someone you can call "friend"

- You don't hold back from doing the things you want to do

- You have the freedom to create

- You feel complete and whole.

In this book, you will gain a new awareness of what it takes to reach the treasure you so desire and richly deserve. You will learn how to use your God-given talents along with abilities cultivated over the years to live in a state of true abundance. You will see that you don't need to compete for it, and that you can bring along your daughters and sons, your friends, lovers, and all of your precious loved ones.

Miracle Of Miracles

Embrace the miracle of *you*. Live in the here and now. Past struggles were there for a reason—maybe you had to learn something from the experience in order to grow into the marvelous woman you are today. Forgive those past hurts, and don't carry them around like dead weight. It's time to align yourself with a new paradigm, one that embraces abundance in every way imaginable.

Perhaps it's difficult for you, at this very moment, to imagine yourself with abundance and prosperity in every aspect of your life. So I'm going to ask you to do something for me. I will ask you to be open to the possibility. Read the following chapters with an open mind and a trusting heart, and see what happens. I think you'll be pleasantly surprised.

Full abundance is attainable. It's reachable … by YOU. It is a realistic dream that you can turn into your personal reality. My prayer and hope is that *Think Your Way To Riches Woman-Style* may serve as your very own passport to the life of your dreams, a life overflowing with the abundance and prosperity you richly deserve. I wish you well on your most exciting journey!

You are invited to continue the relationship at YourAngelChannel.com

1

A History Of Abundance

Nearly every culture tells its own intriguing and beautiful story of a time long, long ago when we all lived abundantly. I believe that every legend has a measure of truth to it, so I feel that this time of abundance truly existed for us. These are not just stories born of wishful thinking. They are tales reflecting how reality was for us as a people. It was a time when there was plenty for everyone, when people lived together in peace, and when cooperation led to wonderful advances for humanity.

Then, whether it had been foreseen and foretold or it happened without any warning whatsoever, this system of abundance began to fall apart. But how could such a thing have happened? What root causes could have led to such disintegration of a dream existence? The causes then were the same causes of our shared problems today: Ego, greed, ungratefulness, desire for dominance, fear.

Little by little, self-confidence was replaced by shame and guilt. Cooperation was replaced by competition. The spirit of giving was lost, replaced by a mentality of want and greed. With these sad changes came a change in our collective reality. Abundance seemed a distant illusion and lack seemed the new reality, with hard labor, endless toil, war and suffering appearing to be humanity's lot.

I certainly won't deny that pain, suffering, and sorrow exist in our world. Nor will I deny that we are equipped to learn valuable spiritual lessons after experiencing sorrow and heartaches. But our everyday reality, day in and day out, year after year, should *not* be dominated by sorrow and pain. Even in our deepest grief, we can tap into the Source Of All Love and feel restored, even for a moment. With time, a measure of healing takes place and, step by step, we can move forward again.

We are people of grace and dignity. We are not poor wretches tossed about the turbulent sea of life. No, we are magnificent miracles! It is high time we believe this, for it is the absolute truth.

So even in the midst of deep pain, there is beauty, even if at first it appears as but a miniscule fragment or a vague recollection of beauty. Even if it's barely perceptible, it's still there. There is also light, joy, life. There is abundance. The fact that we may not see it yet does not mean it is not there. Abundance in some flavor is available to us at all times. The more we align ourselves with this truth, the sooner we will reach the point where abundance is the norm for all of us collectively, just as it was long ago for our sisters and brothers across the ages.

The Ways Of The Earth

Mother Earth knows abundance. Look at the seas, the forests, the jungles, all of which teem with life. Even places that seem barren, such as the darkest depths of the oceans, or the hottest deserts, or the frozen lands, are *full* of life! Nature knows how to create abundance. With a little sunshine, a little water, a little wind, and plenty of Divine Energy, our planet long ago became a sanctuary for life, a place of vibrancy, a home to thousands of species of plant and animal life, all with the ability to recreate and propagate.

Look at a tree. It begins as a tiny seed and grows, year by year, into a tall, stately tree that provides shade for people and animals, plus shelter for creatures like birds and squirrels. It provides fruits for all to enjoy and nourish themselves. It creates new seeds, which scatter and grow into new trees. The ways of the Earth truly are ways of great abundance.

Why is it, then, that throughout history people have not always enjoyed abundance? It seems that for every culture, there have been times of prosperity and times of famine. Times of peace and times of war. Times of plenty and times of lack. Why is this?

In part, we experience "lack" when we distance ourselves. People throughout history have distanced and isolated themselves. This "distancing" is twofold. For one, we separate ourselves from the Earth, which provides for us so abundantly in countless ways. And second, we separate ourselves from the spiritual dimension, which desires nothing more than to help us with our needs. This dual separation has resulted in untold hardships for humanity over the years.

I want to emphasize, though, that it would not be right for us to blame or judge our forefathers and foremothers for the separation that took place. We are an evolving humanity. Just as each of us is where we need to be, right here, right now, so too the people throughout the ages were where *they* needed to be. And if they felt the need to separate, it was because they had to learn specific lessons. Separation was a choice, and a necessary one for growth and evolution.

The Lessons Of Separation

All of humanity's past experiences were necessary to our collective spiritual and practical evolution. Every experience, whether positive or negative, taught us humans a very important lesson. The fact that people distanced themselves from both nature and the Divine simply means that they needed to learn the lessons associated with separation.

Some of the lessons learned fall within these categories:

- Independence
- Isolation
- Self-discovery
- Hardship
- Toil
- Self-reliance
- Ingenuity
- Limitation
- Restriction of roles and norms
- Overcoming challenges
- Pain
- Resourcefulness
- Sacrifice

You are invited to continue the relationship at YourAngelChannel.com

- Necessity
- Power
- Responsibility
- Struggle
- Invention
- Humility
- Yearning
- Incompleteness

History certainly does not need to repeat itself. Some of these lessons we can continue to learn—independence, perhaps, and invention, responsibility, self-discovery—but others we don't need to keep re-learning. We are at a point where we can move forward. We are ready to learn more advanced lessons, which I'll touch upon in the "Future Prosperity" chapter.

Be thankful that our ancestors chose to learn these important lessons. But as the saying goes, "That was then. This is *now*." At this time, we are to learn lessons that involve reuniting with nature and the Divine, without losing our independence and sense of self. We are at a point where we're learning how to be individuals and One, an integral part of the whole, at the same time.

It's History Now

Taking a look at more recent history, say within the last hundred years or so, it's clear that we have been confused about abundance. Many of us, especially those who came from earlier generations, were taught that it's not "lady-like" to expect abundance. How harmful this training has been to women everywhere! Then again, some of us, especially in the newer generations, have been taught to go out there and take, to abandon our femininity and adopt more masculine traits, and to not care one bit if we trample over others in our quest for money, fame, and glory. How harmful this mentality is, too.

Whatever you've been taught, let it go. Forgive the teachers who taught you incorrectly. They didn't know what they were saying, and for many of them, they meant well but simply didn't know any better. They were just repeating what they were taught. They didn't have the discernment to see the truth yet, or the courage to question and challenge what they were taught. Sometimes it takes many generations before truth and wisdom break through.

As I've stated before, abundance is your birthright! So naturally it's lady-like, or woman-like, to expect it. But you don't have to compete for it, or take it from others, or acquire it by force. The truth is that abundance comes in many forms and is all around us, and you are entitled to it without needing to compromise yourself or hurt others. That type of behavior is "old history." It's time to leave history behind and start a new way of perceiving and achieving abundance.

2

Where Are We Now?

We certainly stand at an interesting and exciting point in history. No longer do we women need to "prove" ourselves. No longer do we have to be restricted to certain roles and norms. Today we are fully emancipated, which means that we are free to be who we are, who we want to be, without having to compromise ourselves. We are free to enjoy the abundance that is our birthright.

It is, indeed, a momentous time in our history, a rich and colorful history that goes way back to ancient times and eras that today we can hardly fathom. Our history books just don't have the capacity and breadth to cover it all. Collectively as a human race, and also spiritually, and just as significantly as individuals, we've been evolving for a very long time, and our evolution has brought us to precisely this place and time. What a glorious time to be alive on Mother Earth!

You are now at the point where you are beginning to realize that you make your own choices. If the path before you is unclear, the reason is simple: the road is waiting to be built by you. No longer do you have to walk a predefined path. *You* get to define it. You get to call the shots. It's no longer about shoulds, haftas, or even "it's always been done that way." It's about applying your God-given creativity to sculpt your life, in your way. This is true, bona fide abundance.

In The Driver's Seat

You hold the steering wheel now. Where do you want to go? What do you wish to do? How will you fill the moments that collectively make up your life? If it seems like a daunting task, don't worry. You don't need to map out every second of the rest of your life. Start with today. Begin with this morning, afternoon, or evening. What will you do with this slice of time? What choices will you make today? What outlook do you choose to adopt at this particular moment?

The way you create a meaningful, abundant life for yourself is by stopping every so often and taking stock of where you are and where you want to be. If you're not quite where you wish to be, then simply make a little change. Take a step or two today that will align you with the path you want to be traveling along. Don't worry about tomorrow, or next month. You have today; what will you do this day to move you into abundance?

The past has proven valuable to us. During every era, humanity has learned something critical to our evolution, as a species and as spiritual beings. As I alluded to in the previous chapter, even the mistakes of our ancestors have taught us well. We needn't be afraid of making mistakes, for when we do make them, with the right attitude we can turn them into marvelous learning opportunities.

We must thank the people who walked this planet before us, because their combined successes and failures, trials and triumphs, acts of kindness and "aha" moments have brought us to this point in history. And this is, by many measures, one of the greatest times to be alive. It is the birth of an era of new consciousness when we are free to make individual choices based not on selfishness but on confidence that our unique contributions add so much to our shared existence.

Within this new consciousness, we know that there is enough for everyone. There is no need to hoard or to hide goods from others. Solutions are reachable, and each of us is capable of dreaming up real answers for old problems. By being free to be who we truly are, each of us marches forward with a common goal of making abundance an attainable dream for every person on this planet.

A Time To Choose

So it comes down to this. Do we conduct business as usual, or do we seize this marvelous opportunity we're given to choose a better way, an enlightened way, an empowering way? Truly it's an exciting time to be alive. Things are no longer cast in stone. Really, they never were, but today the illusion is fully revealed. Today we know that we create our reality by the thoughts we think, the words we say, the choices we make, the actions we take.

You can change whatever you wish. You can change your attitudes, your self-perception, your way of relating to others, your direction, your focus. All of these changes are well within the realm of possibility. This is a critical point in time, because what we choose now will manifest as our future destiny, perhaps more quickly than at any other time in history. Throughout the world people are going through the process of choice. They are choosing between doing what they've always done and what they could be doing instead. Many (millions, in fact) are choosing to make a little change here, and a bigger shift there, in order to live their personal truth.

Less Can Be More

More than anything else, the term "riches" means a certain quality of life that you desire. For some women, reaching abundance means *scaling back*, not adding more to their already full plates. It could mean:

- Spending fewer hours at work in order to enjoy more time at home, with family and friends, or pursuing personal interests.

- Selling, donating, or discarding some possessions and moving into a smaller, not larger, home. This can then result in less time spent on cleaning and maintenance, and more appreciation for the fewer possessions you choose to keep.

- Preparing and consuming simpler, more organic meals. This could mean less meat, fewer processed foods, and more fresh fruits and vegetables. Perhaps smaller portions, too. Or switching over to several smaller meals a day instead of two or three huge meals.

- Scaling back on social obligations. Choosing the friends and events that are truly enjoyable, and not feeling guilty about skipping parties or releasing some friendships.

- Choosing a more basic approach to motherhood, one that involves more time spent with your child, more hugs, and more laughter, and less material possessions, less structured days, and fewer expectations.

These are ways some women have chosen to simplify their lives in order to enjoy greater riches. Now, back to you. What type of life do you envision? What abundance do you seek? What choices will you make today that will create the destiny you desire? The time is ripe for designing your life on your terms. Seize the day!

3

Future Prosperity

One of the wonderful aspects of abundance is that the more you do for your true self, the more you do for every woman and man out there. Your future prosperity, which begins this instant, sets the tone for the future prosperity of everyone around you, everyone you encounter. And through this ripple effect, with each woman creating her life of abundance, pretty soon it spreads in every direction and *everyone* is positively affected.

A beautiful dream, isn't it? Well, this dream is turning into reality for more and more women each day. Why not you? Future prosperity is not merely wishful thinking; it is the direction we as a common humanity are marching towards, a future where every person counts and individual contributions add to everyone's abundance.

The Wheels Are Set Into Motion

I want to share with you some of the beautiful ways courageous women are creating their own future prosperity as well as prosperity and abundance for others:

Lucinda Yates: After a divorce and financial hardships, this Maine-based mother found herself homeless. She knew she didn't want to stay in that situation. Family and friends helped her and her daughter move into a modest home. There, Lucinda unleashed her creativity and launched her own line of fashion jewelry.

After running her business for several years, she came up with a brilliant idea—sell one-of-a-kind handcrafted pins with house motifs to raise funds to help the homeless. That idea has grown even further, and today Lucinda creates a wide variety of pins that groups utilize to raise funds for a number of causes. What a wonderful way to tap into her abundance and simultaneously help others reach their abundance!

Wangari Muta Maathai: Thanks to this woman, more than 30 *million* trees have been planted throughout Kenya in an effort to help the environment by creating a green belt. In the process of helping the environment, Wangari empowers women, as they are the ones primarily involved in this phenomenal grassroots effort.

She is a woman of many firsts: the first woman in East Africa to earn a doctorate degree. The first woman to chair the Department of Veterinary Anatomy at the University of Nairobi. The first African woman to win the Nobel Peace Prize, which she received in 2004 for furthering sustainability, democracy, and peace. By pursuing her own passion for education, women's issues, and the environment, Wangari has made an incredible difference for her whole country and inspired others to do as she has done. She is affectionately called "The Tree Mother Of Africa."

Pamela Melroy and Peggy Whitson: In October of 2007, history was made when these two women met up in space. As the space shuttle and the international space station docked in orbit, these two women were in charge. Pamela served as the shuttle *Discovery* commander and Peggy was the commander at the space station.

This was the first time in the 46 years of spaceflight history that two women led missions simultaneously. To think that once upon a time, NASA would not accept women astronauts. Now, not even the sky's the limit!

These are but four among millions of women who are creating their future prosperity *now*. More accurately, they are achieving their abundance now, and in the process they are creating a future of prosperity for everyone—both present and future generations. They are not afraid to live fully and follow their dreams. Along the way, they shape the course of history, doing their part to make sure people are treated with dignity, basic social needs are met, the environment is preserved, and future generations have unlimited opportunities available to them.

You are invited to continue the relationship at YourAngelChannel.com

What about you? You can follow your passion, too. You are every bit as capable as these women are to make a difference. Follow your dreams, claim your right to abundance in your life, and watch how wonderful things begin to happen. Not only for you, but for everyone your life touches, now and in the future. You can alter the direction of humanity. You can change history. It begins with you and your desire to reach your abundance.

The Lessons We're Learning For Our Future

In a previous chapter I listed some of the lessons of separation that our ancestors chose to learn. Now we stand at a different point in time, and we're poised to learn exciting lessons in new areas, including:

- Cooperation
- Compassion
- Peace
- Re-connection with nature
- Reconnecting to the Divine
- Simplicity
- Grace
- Laughter
- Joy
- Permission
- Community
- Individual pursuits
- Possibilities
- Choices
- Concern for the welfare of others

You are invited to continue the relationship at YourAngelChannel.com

- Love
- Self-respect
- Dignity
- Dreams
- Creating our reality
- Abundance

Face the future with courage in your heart, a sense of anticipation, joy in your soul, and a sense of adventure! It will be fun. You are ready to start creating your future of abundance *now*. There is no need to wait. You are equipped with marvelous gifts to make it happen. Trust yourself, and begin the journey.

4

Think Your Way To Abundance

What are you thinking right now? This very moment, what thoughts are being formed in your mind? Listen to them. Are your thoughts lifting you up or bringing you down? Truly, we create our reality by the thoughts we develop. How many times have you heard yourself or a loved one utter one of these statements:

- I'll never get it right!

- I can't do this.

- I'm no good at it.

- I wasn't made for this.

- It's impossible!

Your mind is extremely powerful. Your body, right down to the cellular level, listens to what your mind says. Your emotions also respond to what your mind's telling you, consciously and subconsciously. Even your energetic self responds to what you tell yourself. If your mind says "I can't," the rest of you responds accordingly. Your body holds you back, because after all, you've just told yourself you can't. Your energy level goes down, too, in agreement with what your mind is stating. And your emotions work to create a feeling that goes along with that "can't" mentality, once again holding you back.

Now, take a moment to rethink what you were just thinking. Can you reframe it into a positive form? Can you modify your thoughts, ever so slightly, to affirm, uplift, and uphold you? Of course you can. It doesn't take much to go from statements that hold you back to words that bring you abundance:

- I'll get it right!

- I can do this.

- I'm good at it.

- I was made for this.

You are invited to continue the relationship at YourAngelChannel.com

- It's possible and doable!

You must be vigilant, and persistent, and above all gentle with yourself. Your pattern of thinking evolved over a lifetime. Don't expect to change it overnight. Do expect, however, to make slight modifications, little by little, so that you'll gradually and surely adopt a new way of thinking. This is your first important step to achieving the abundance that is your birthright.

In the same way that your mind affects your body, emotions, and energy, these components that make up who you are influence your mind. When you feel happy and fulfilled, for example, these emotions help your mind think positive thoughts. When you feel afraid, your mind likes to come up with scenarios that give you a reason to fear.

Likewise, if your body is tense or sore, your mind is distracted by this. When you are relaxed, then your mind is free to be creative and wonderfully constructive. Our various components are not separate at all. Mind, body, spirit, and energy are interconnected, ever influencing one another.

For this reason, your mind will benefit from you being in a relaxed state. To foster thoughts that will lift you up and prepare you to receive the abundance you deserve, get yourself into a relaxed and receptive state. The following exercise will help you to relax your body, generate good feelings, get your energy flowing, and clear your mind to make room for positive, empowering thoughts.

Exercise 1: Guided Imagery For Relaxation & Positive Thinking

Find a quiet moment, and create a peaceful state around you. Turn off the TV, radio, computer, and anything else that's noisy or that might distract you. Take several deep breaths. With each inhale, envision the word "LOVE." What does love look like? Does it have a color? A spectrum of colors? How does it feel? What beautiful images are you breathing in?

With every exhale, envision the word "PEACE." Picture it as an energy that calms everything it touches. Feel yourself become more relaxed and at peace with every breath you release. Feel your environment growing more and more serene, more peaceful. When you feel ready, begin the following guided imagery:

My mind is calm and open. My heart is calm and receptive. My body is relaxed and aware. I am at peace with myself and with the world around me. I release love, joy, and peace. I feel love, joy, and peace return to me.

Within my mind, I create a vast ocean. This beautiful, clear ocean is the immensity of God's love. The ocean is the potential of all creation, and the original force moving into my world.

I see myself standing tall, calmly confident, facing the gentle waves that softly kiss my being and invite me to swim in the abundance of God's love. I walk toward the ocean and slip slowly into the warm waves. I float, and feel safe in the buoyant waves. I breathe in God's love. The ocean of love seeps into my pores, and circulates through my body and brain.

You are invited to continue the relationship at YourAngelChannel.com

I slowly sink to the depth of all potential, and transform into a dolphin. I am the different creature who lives in this depth and knows the feeling of love and safety. I am free. I feel rich. I am love. I am abundance.

As the dolphin, I swim through God's abundant potential to imbibe and embody the fullness of this Love experience. Now I am silent and let my experience unfold.

Let yourself to spend as much time as you like immersed in this experience. When you are ready, come back to where you are, breathe deeply, and allow your body to move as needed.

You have successfully elevated yourself to a higher state. Without physically going anywhere, you've traveled in your mind and spirit to attain a level of relaxation that fosters positive thinking. With your spirit enriched, your mind refreshed, and your body energized, you now completely feel embraced by the abundant energy that flows through you and the Universe, making us ALL connected as one…

Before you move on to the next exercise, give yourself a present: remain for a while in the state you've just created for yourself. Feel how strong you are in mind, body, and soul. Feel soothing love flow through every cell of your body, from the top of your head through your middle and out through your fingers and toes. This is the *real* you.

When you feel ready, move on to Exercise 2. Have a glass of water or a cup of herbal tea first. Enjoy a little break.

Exercise 2: Clarity Of Thought

Now that you are relaxed and in a positive state of mind, you are in a position to tune your thoughts and align them to your greater good. This is important for two main reasons. First, every thought is, in essence, a prayer you make. And just as importantly, *your* thoughts create *your* reality.

There are times when we don't get what we want, or what we believe we want, simply because we're not sufficiently clear about our true intention. Look at these examples of "muddled thinking;" do you see how each would send mixed messages out to the universe?

- I so want to go to Hawaii … but I don't want to get on an airplane.

- I'd love to take this class … but I'm not sure I'd do well in it.

- I want to introduce myself to that group over there … but I'm afraid they'll reject me.

Do you see how each thought, each wish, each desire, each prayer, actually sabotages itself? There's one step forward … and one step back. You'll find that fear and doubt are the biggest thought-scramblers around.

You *want* Hawaii … but you *don't want* a plane ride, so guess what? Hawaii's not going to happen (unless, of course, you get there by sea). You *want* to take a class and learn something new and interesting … but you *don't want* to face the struggles and challenges that may come with it. Muddled thinking sabotages your life and holds you back from doing what you really would like to do.

To avoid getting into this quandary, practice *clear thinking.* To get a better idea of what your goal is here, take a look at dogs. Yes, dogs! You immediately know what a dog wants, because he'll tell you in no uncertain terms by the way he focuses his attention on something so completely. When a dog wants to eat, his attention is right there in the food bowl, a hundred percent. When a dog wants to play, he'll bring you a tennis ball and drop it right on your lap. You understand what your dog friend wants because there's complete clarity of thought and intention on his part. We can learn much from our wonderful animal friends.

All right, now it's your turn. Practice clearing your thoughts through the following:

Picture in your mind one thing that you'd like to do. It can be anything of your choosing.

1. *See yourself doing this one thing. Don't deviate from the scenario—picture yourself doing the activity of your choice, and hold this picture in your mind.*

2. *If you find the picture evolving into something else, gently bring the original image back into your mind's eye view and hold it there.*

3. *If you find fear or doubt trying to butt in and change the picture, gently push these away and return to your original scenario.*

You are invited to continue the relationship at YourAngelChannel.com

4. *Hold on to your original thought for several minutes. Keep going back to it every time you feel it starting to change into something else.*

5. *Once you're able to firmly hold that thought in your mind, internalize it.*

6. *Make it real—experience this thought as if it were a scene in your life or an event that's actually happening. Do you notice any accompanying emotions or pleasant body sensations?*

This exercise trains you to hold on to one specific desired thought while pushing all others—especially distractions, doubts, and fears—away from you. What you're doing is protecting this thought and holding it above all others. The more you practice this exercise, the better able you'll become at keeping your thoughts clear. With more focused thoughts, you'll find that you will get what you desire more frequently … and more easily.

In this exercise you learned how to block fear and doubt. In the next exercise, you'll learn how to rid guilt and shame from your thinking.

Exercise 3: Purity Of Thought—Remove Guilt & Shame Emotions

As we discussed earlier, your mind, feelings, body, energy, and spirit interact with one another regularly. Not one system is isolated from the rest. Your body affects your mind, your mind affects your energy, your emotions affect your body, and so on.

Because of how we've been raised, and perhaps because of the particular value system we've been taught, we don't allow ourselves to think thoughts we deem "inappropriate." Many of us women (and some men, too) have been raised to believe that it's shameful to brag about ourselves, or to make a ton of money, or to take care of our own needs. We've therefore associated guilt and shame with certain thoughts, making them "taboo."

It's time rectify the situation and purify our thoughts. Despite what we've been taught, the truth is that it's *not* shameful to earn our wealth, or to take care of ourselves, or to openly talk about something we did well. These are *not* "bad." On the contrary, each of these can serve us quite well. So it's high time, ladies, to purge our minds from the mistaken notion that specific thoughts are bad, when in reality they aren't.

Here is your exercise. Start with these examples:

- *Filthy rich*

- *Stuck-up showoff*

- *Indulgent narcissist*

There are strong negative connotations associated with these phrases, aren't there? Let's try to change that. How can we purge these phrases of their negative meanings and instead assign positive feelings to them? How would you turn these negatives into positives? Here are some ideas:

- *Happy wealthy*

- *Confident achiever*

- *Person who takes care of herself*

See how the negative connotations are gone? A person who has the financial means to take care of herself, her loved ones, AND the causes she believes in is not filthy rich—she's happy wealthy. And the woman who reaches her dreams is not a stuck-up showoff; she's a confident achiever.

There is no need to keep thinking the way you've always been taught if that way of thinking holds you back from your abundance and prosperity. If you've been looking at the world through clouded glass, remove the glass to see things more clearly. You will then begin to see yourself and others as beautiful spiritual beings rather than stereotyped caricatures.

What other terms can you come up with to replace erroneous, guilt-ridden, or shame-based thinking? What freeing, true, and empowering thoughts can you create instead? Jot down the "before" and "after" thoughts. Focus on the improved "after" versions:

These terms replace "shame-based thinking" and serve me infinitely better:

It's no secret that many of us have trouble justifying money in our lives, or even seeing it as good. Here's your opportunity to remove any negative thoughts you may have ascribed to money and release the hold these thoughts have over you. Money, in and of itself, is not "bad." It's just a means to an end. Money can be very, very good. It can feed the

You are invited to continue the relationship at YourAngelChannel.com

hungry around the world, put food on your own table, supply books to schoolchildren, or build your dream home. Each of these is a good thing. Making, having, or spending money aren't bad. It's what you choose to do regarding money that makes the difference. And it is your choice.

Here's one more activity for you to do before we move on. Take a look at the following table. See how each phrase is transformed into something pure, something that doesn't carry negative baggage? Practice transforming other phrases as well.

Negative Thinking	Positive Shift In Thinking
Money is gone	Money is present in my life
Money is dirty	Money is clean energy
Money is not mine	Money is mine
Money is absent from my life	Money is present fro me
Rich people are snobs	Rich people are friendly
Rich people are unscrupulous	Rich people are conscientious

Through these previous exercises you have worked on the power of thought. You have learned how to:

- Get yourself into a relaxed state that leads to positive thinking

- Maintain clear, focused thoughts that reflect what you really want, not what you don't want

- Push fear and doubt away when they creep in to sabotage your thoughts

- Purify your thoughts so that guilt and shame aren't tainting them

- Free yourself to think thoughts for your personal wellbeing without feeling "ashamed" of doing so.

Practice these exercises often. Ultimately they will shift your pattern of thinking so that you can start to bring abundance into your life through your thoughts, instead of pushing abundance and prosperity away. These exercises will serve you well as they help you learn how to think your way to abundance!

Today's Affirmation: I am free to think thoughts that will better who I am and express my true self. I am beautiful inside and out, and I am well capable. As I swim in the ocean of God's love, I remember that all things are possible.

Each day my thoughts become clearer. My thoughts are pure. Each day, my thoughts create my reality. I am thinking my way to joy, light, love, prosperity, and abundance in every sense imaginable. Not even the sky's the limit! I am free to think without limits.

You are invited to continue the relationship at YourAngelChannel.com

My Personal Thoughts

_____

_____

_____

_____

_____

_____

_____

_____

_____

_____

_____

_____

_____

You are invited to continue the relationship at YourAngelChannel.com

Today's Action Item

Think About It

- Before something was created—a new invention, a solution, a corporation, a beautiful song, a medical cure—someone, somewhere, dared to think it possible.

- You can choose to think thoughts that will hold you back, or thoughts that will advance you forward. What is your choice?

- Your focus does, indeed, ultimately create your personal reality.

5

What Do You Desire To Change?

Each of us desires to change something different within ourselves and our lives. So let's get specific here, and personal. What, exactly, do *you* wish to change? Do you want:

- More money?

- More time?

- Better relationships?

- A more rewarding job?

- Better health?

- Greater happiness?

- More self-confidence?

- More love?

- Greater serenity?

To start with, pick one, or two, or all of the above. If none of the above describes what you wish to change in your life, then write down what it is that *you* want. Don't be shy. Be honest with yourself as you search your heart for your desire. This is an excellent place to start. Once you have a handle on what you wish to change, it's time to delve deeper and get specific.

Let's say you picked "more money." Ask yourself probing questions, such as these:

- *Why did I make this choice?*

- *What will I do with more money?*

- *How will I put it to use?*

- *What benefits will having more money bring?*

- *How will my life be more abundant?*

Write down your answers to these questions. The more specific you are, the more clarity you bring to the situation. And the clearer you are about what you want, the easier it will be for you to achieve your abundance in this area.

It's vital that you get to the core of the matter. Continuing with our example, find out what, exactly, you *desire* that is making you wish for more money. Dig deeply; what's the motivation behind the change you wish to make? Do you desire to have a nicer home? A more interesting wardrobe? The ability to pay all of your bills every month? A vacation? More funds to give away to charity? New clothes for the kids? A computer? The monetary means to help out a family member or friend? Dinner out at a restaurant once in a while? Financial security?

Money by itself isn't worth much. It's just a bunch of bills upon which words, letters, and illustrations have been printed. You can't eat it, you can't wear it, and you can't make someone feel better by waving a dollar bill in front of her. Money alone is quite useless.

The real question here is, what form of abundance do you seek where money is the avenue to attaining it? Think about this for a moment. Feel free to write down the various thoughts that come to you:

Some of the forms of abundance I seek:

_____

_____

_____

_____

_____

_____

_____

_____

_____

All right, let's move on now. Take a look again at the list above, the one at the start of this chapter. Is it a more rewarding job that you want? Why? What would be "more rewarding" for you? What aspects of your current job do you want to keep? What do you want to change? Again, getting specific let's you get clearer about what you desire.

In the following exercises, you'll learn how to determine what you want to change, and why it is that you want to make that change. You'll delve more deeply to get to the heart of the matter. And you'll see how desire can be a powerful motivator that you can use to your advantage.

Exercise 1: Check With Your Intuition

Your intuition is a mighty powerful and wise counselor. It can reveal many things, if you allow it to. By checking with your intuition, you can find out which areas of your life you feel dissatisfied with, as well as what you're happy about. Your intuition can give you solid clues about what you'd like to change. Giving yourself enough time, try the following steps to connect to your intuition and learn to trust it fully:

1. *Take three sheets of standard 8 ½" x 11" paper. Fold these three sheets into quarters.*

2. *In each quarter, write down one word from this list:*
   - *Spiritual*
   - *Mental*
   - *Emotional*
   - *Physical*
   - *Career*
   - *Family*
   - *Friends*
   - *Relationships*
   - *Time*
   - *Money*
   - *Balance*
   - *Fun*

3. *Cut out each square.*

4. *For each category, write down as many aspects of your life as you can think of. On the front of each square, write down what you consider to be your blessings within this category. On the back, write down areas where you feel there's room for improvement. For example, under "Physical" you might write down "strong, healthy, enjoy dancing, hugging my child, and working with the earth in my garden" as some of your blessings. You might list "would like to exercise more"*

or "I want to spend more time working in my garden" on the back of the sheet as areas that need improvement. These are just examples, of course. Come up with your own.

5. *Shuffle your 12 squares. With your eyes closed so that what you wrote on each piece of paper won't accidentally sway you, lay them out in front of you. Ask yourself, "Which area of my life would I like to work on first?"*

6. *Take a deep breath and keep your eyes closed. Using your intuition only, reach out and pick up a square.*

7. *Open your eyes. Read which category you've chosen. This is the category you are to work on first with regards to making changes in your life. Does it feel right?*

8. *Write down the numeral one on this square, and circle the number. Set this square aside.*

9. *Now review the remaining 11 squares. Pick up each one, in the order of your choice, allowing your intuition to guide you. Hold the first one in your hands a moment. Read what you listed under "blessings." Next read what you wrote for "needs improvement." How does this category feel to you? Do you feel pretty happy with your life in this area? Or do you feel more dissatisfied than satisfied? Would you like to change something within this category, or are you pleased with the way things are?*

10. *After spending some time pondering these questions, rate this category with one of the following headings:*

   - *Fine as is*

- *Needs eventual improvement*
- *Needs immediate improvement*

11. Repeat Steps 9 and 10 with the remaining squares.

12. Stack the squares according to the heading they fall under (fine as is, needs eventual improvement, needs immediate improvement).

13. Pick up the stack of "fine as is." Read what you wrote down for each category. Say a prayer of thanks for what each square represents, either out loud or quietly to yourself, whichever you prefer. Feel the warmth in your heart and the tickle in your soul as you internalize the blessings each square represents. When you are ready, discard this pile. The squares are gone, but the warm feelings remain with you.

14. Next take the stack you've labeled "needs eventual improvement." Read the blessings you wrote for each one. Again, give thanks, and feel the warmth and joy of these blessings and your gratitude permeate your whole being.

15. After you've given thanks, ask your intuition to rank each square. Assign a number to each square; "number one" is the category you'll work on first, three months from today. Then you'll move on to "number two," and so on, working your way through the stack.

16. Put the "needs eventual improvement" pile in a place where you'll find it three months from now, perhaps with your daytime planner or in your nightstand drawer. Mark your calendar—in three months, you'll begin processing these

You are invited to continue the relationship at YourAngelChannel.com

squares to figure out what you want to change within each category, and how to go about enacting this change.

17. Take a deep breath and utter a prayer of thanks.

18. Now, turn your attention to the remaining pile, the "needs immediate improvement" stack. This is what you'll be working on first. Pick up this stack, along with the square you identified as "number one" in Step 8. Place this stack in a prominent spot, such as on your nightstand or someplace else where it'll remain in plain sight.

You've done great work! Now take a deep breath, and release it, all the way out. Again, breathe in and envision the beautiful energy of LOVE entering with your breath and through every pore of your body. Then breathe out, and picture a peaceful energy touching everything that's around you. Feel your mind quieting, your body relaxing, and your soul reaching a wonderful sense of peace.

Take a well-deserved break. You have done your work for today. Tomorrow, you will find the pile that you've left in a prominent place and you will begin Exercise 2. For now, take it easy and enjoy a bit of quiet reflection time. Drink plenty of pure, clean water. Enjoy a walk or special time with loved ones. Get a good night's rest.

You are invited to continue the relationship at YourAngelChannel.com

Exercise 2: What's At The Heart Of Your Desired Change?

In Exercise 1, you allowed your intuition to guide you to the areas that you wish to change most in your life. Now, let's get to the heart of the matter. Why do you wish to transform these areas?

Find the stack that you created yesterday and placed in a prominent spot, your "needs immediate improvement" pile. Locate the "number one" square. Read the category, the blessings, and the items under "needs improvement."

Ponder this category for a while. If you wish, meditate or pray about this area of your life. When you are ready, write down your answers to the following:

I feel I want to make changes in this area because…

_____

_____

_____

_____

_____

_____

You are invited to continue the relationship at YourAngelChannel.com

_____

_____

*By making these changes, I believe that things will improve for me in the
following ways:*

_____

_____

_____

_____

_____

_____

_____

_____

Here are some ways I can make changes to get my desired results:

_____

_____

_____

_____

_____

_____

_____

_____

_____

Once you've pondered your answers to the "number one" square, move on to another square. Use your intuition to decide which category to evaluate next. Repeat this exercise by writing down your thoughts about changes for each category.

There is no need to rush. Take your time. If you want to process all in an afternoon or a day, you may. If you'd rather work on one at a time—one a day, one a week—then by all means do so. Do what is most comfortable for you, what fits into your schedule, what feels right. Let your intuition be your guide.

Exercise 3: Get Motivated!

You can boil it all down to one word: success. The bottom line is that you want to succeed at being happy, enjoying life, being all that you can be. Well, did you know that to succeed, you need something inside yourself to motivate your spirit? It's true. What you think about in your thoughts, feel in your heart, and want in life will activate the power of desire and bring what you are wishing for. When you begin this process, the change that you desire will materialize in time. For now, don't worry about how long it takes to make the changes you wish for; instead, focus on what *motivates* you to make these changes.

Start with your "number one" square. You've already come up with reasons you want to make a change, and you've listed ways that your life will improve with these changes made. Take it one step further. Imagine that you're there. Tell yourself that these changes have already been made, and that you now are where you previously desired to be. You have attained the success you have been dreaming about. Envision yourself as completely and totally being there.

Now, internalize this image. How does it feel to have made the desired change? How does it feel to live in the success you've dreamed about, to float in it, to be completely immersed in its wonderful hold? Pay attention to the feelings that emerge. Visualize your reality in this new realm. Hang on to the feelings you come across while experiencing this reality.

These feelings that you evoked are key. Did you feel excitement? Confidence? Contentment? Boundless joy? Write down whatever pleasant feelings you noticed. These feelings are key because they will motivate you to make the changes you wish to bring to your life. By holding on to the excitement or the joy or the thrill or the bliss you experience when you think about what will be, you will fuel your transformation. Let these feelings feed your soul and motivate you to make the change.

You are invited to continue the relationship at <u>YourAngelChannel.com</u>

Repeat this exercise with each of the other categories in your "needs immediate improvement" pile. Every day, spend some moments picturing yourself having achieved your heart's desire. Feel the emotions that these visualizations evoke. Internalize the feelings, and let them propel you forward in your mission to achieve the change you desire.

The three previous exercises will help you to mature in your desire for change. They will take you from mere wishful thinking to focused, intentional thinking coupled with commitment, a very powerful combination. They will teach you to get to the heart of the matter and generate feelings of anticipation, excitement, and passion that will motivate you to stay on course and achieve your desired outcome. Celebrate—you are on your way!

Today's Affirmation: Because I have chosen to be here on this wonderful journey called life, in the physical realm, on Mother Earth, I desire certain goals and realities for myself. They give me something to reach for, something to strive for, and reason to grow. As I grow and transform, I become who I truly am beyond the façade: a beautiful participant of life, a powerful spiritual being, a dignified human being, an empowered and fulfilled woman.

My desire for change reflects the love and respect I hold for myself. I know that I walk this life journey to learn more about myself, to discover who I am, to reach my potential, to live abundantly. My desire for change is natural and good. It propels me to become who I am meant to be.

My Personal Thoughts

_____

_____

_____

_____

_____

_____

_____

_____

_____

_____

_____

Today's Action Item

_____

_____

_____

_____

_____

_____

_____

_____

_____

_____

_____

_____

Think About It

- While some people are stuck in a fantasy world of wishing things were different, you are empowering yourself to figure out exactly what you want to change and why you desire to make this change.

- Knowing the motivation behind your heart's desire gives you the fuel you need to keep moving in the right direction.

- A desire for change is the seed from which sprouts true, life-enhancing transformation.

Envision Your Riches

In the previous chapter, you practiced envisioning yourself succeeding at bringing about the changes you desire. Visualization is a very powerful technique, used by everyone from athletes to actors to brain surgeons, believe it or not. When you visualize yourself doing, completing, or attaining something before it comes to pass, you're accomplishing more than you might realize:

- You're going through a mental practice run

- You're planting seeds that will grow into the results you're visualizing

- You're aligning yourself, including your thoughts, emotions, and energy field, with the reality you desire.

I'm certain you've heard it said many times: practice makes perfect. This holds true whether you're practicing in the physical Earth realm, or whether you're doing a mental run-through. When you visualize, you see results before they happen, and this prepares you for the success that is sure to follow when you stay focused on your path.

The whole of you doesn't really know the difference between real and imagined. When you picture an event in your mind, and you hold that mental image in place, the cells of your body react to this image as though it were truly happening. Your energy field responds, imprinting this envisioned successful outcome into your psyche. In other words, when you see it in your mind enough times, you *believe it*. And when you believe it with every fiber of your being, it becomes first your truth and then your reality.

In this chapter I'm going to give you permission to envision your wildest dreams. What do you want for your life? What have you been told that you can't have? Whether it was intentional or unintentional, people from your past and present may have given you the impression that certain riches are beyond your reach. I'm here to dispel that myth. That which you desire is within your reach, and you are entitled to it. Believe it.

Riches come in various forms. In the first exercise you'll define "riches" according to your terms. Then you'll move on to "seeing" these riches in your life, in your possession. And third, you will take a step towards bringing a specific flavor of riches into your sphere of reality. As you work through these exercises, keep in mind that envisioning your riches enables you to:

You are invited to continue the relationship at <u>YourAngelChannel.com</u>

- See the results before they actually happen

- Compare possible outcomes that different courses of action might yield

- See yourself starting, doing, and completing what you need to do to attain your riches, well before taking your first step on the physical realm

- Start building a bridge that will take you from your desires to your richer reality

- Go from dreaming about your riches to reaching them.

The clearer you can see your riches in your thoughts, the sooner you will bring them into your life. When you take the time to visualize your riches—however you choose to define them—in detail and with specificity, you lay the groundwork for having that experience of abundance on the Earth plane. You practice in your mind, and you build a bridge from this particular moment to the future of your desires.

Exercise 1: Define Your Riches

"Riches" is a beautiful word. It refers to the abundance you desire in your life. Riches can be defined as:

- Days filled with joy and laughter

- A simpler life

- Quality time with people you love

- A job or vocation you thoroughly enjoy

- Healthy finances

- Enough time to do the things you enjoy

- Good health

- Happiness

- A warm, cozy home

- Material possessions

- Financial wealth

- Friendship

- Family

- Wisdom

- A strong connection to the spiritual realm

- Creative energy

You are invited to continue the relationship at YourAngelChannel.com

Now it's time to discover and define your personal riches. Let yourself daydream. Find a quiet, comfortable place and relax for a few moments. Pay attention to your breath as you inhale, exhale, inhale, exhale. Listen to birds singing, children playing, the gentle notes of wind chimes, or whatever other pleasant sounds you notice. Enjoy the moment. Enjoy being in the now.

Let your mind wander to that which you enjoy and love most. Allow these thoughts to swirl around in creative waves of energy. Let these thoughts float as colors and abstract ideas. Enjoy feeling the process of creativity well up inside you. Let the good feelings that emanate merge with your thoughts.

Now allow your thoughts to form fully. Let them take shape while you keep focusing on that which you enjoy and love the most. Images will begin to appear. Go into these images. Pass through them and look around. Note what they are, and how they make you feel. Pay close attention to those that make you feel the best.

When you are ready, transform these images and ideas into words. Complete the following thought:

Based on what I am intuiting, envisioning, and experiencing in my mind, heart, soul, emotions, and energy field, I believe that my riches are…

_____

_____

_____

You are invited to continue the relationship at YourAngelChannel.com

_____

_____

_____

_____

_____

_____

_____

_____

_____

_____

What you just wrote is your personal definition of "riches" that you'll be using in the following exercise. Before continuing, spend a few moments immersed in your thoughts and feelings associated with your very special definition of riches.

Exercise 2: Envision These Riches In Your Life

Continue with your fruitful daydreaming. Now that you've written down your own definition of riches, your next step is to picture yourself immersed in this abundance. Close your eyes, and remain in your semi-meditative state. Envision the riches you defined in exercise 1 as being in your life right now. Hold this vision in your mind's eye.

Then, immerse yourself in this vision. Feel the emotions that the riches evoke. Experience your riches with your five senses—touch, smell, taste, sight, sound. Internalize the experience. Feel your abundance using your sixth sense.

Linger within this fantastic picture in your mind. What does it feel like to bask in abundance? What does the picture of abundance look like to you? How do you look immersed in abundance? Give your particular brand of riches a color. What color have you assigned to your abundance? Swim in silky smooth energy made of this color. Feel the warmth and invigoration of your abundance.

Exercise 3: Bring Riches Into Your Life

You have now defined your riches, and you've envisioned them as an integral part of your life. You've envisioned yourself swimming in a sea of abundance. Next, you will actually *bring* riches into your life.

For this exercise, we'll work with a particular flavor of riches universally valued: *laughter*. By the end of this exercise, you'll enjoy more abundant laughter in your life, and you'll experience its healing, therapeutic power. Once you've worked through this exercise, you can repeat it using another form of riches of your choice.

You are to do one or more of the following. Start with one today. Then, do at least one more before the end of the week. If you wish, do them all, or if you prefer, choose the ones you'd like to do, and make it a point to complete these within seven days:

1. *Bring home an uplifting funny movie or show. It could be a classic, such as **I Love Lucy**, or something contemporary, whatever you prefer. Schedule time to watch your movie or show today. If you have time, watch a full-length film. If you're a little pressed for time today, then a half-hour segment will do the trick. As you watch the antics, give yourself permission to laugh out loud, without reservation. Feel laughter emanate from deep within your belly. Feel yourself connect directly to the place where your powerful spiritual self dwells. Feel like a kid again!*

2. *Call a friend or other loved one known for her or his good sense of humor. No need for excuses or long explanations; call this person and tell them that you need to laugh today, and they're the first person who came to mind. This will lift the other person up as well as you. Spend fifteen minutes or so engaged in light, fun conversation with this person. Laugh together. By the end of your phone call, you and your friend will feel lighter and more joyous.*

You are invited to continue the relationship at YourAngelChannel.com

3.   *Listen to an audio recording of a funny comedian who knows how to make us laugh at ourselves while affirming the special, sacred qualities of life. Or watch a taped recording of one of their performances. Perhaps a skit by Bill Cosby or Ellen Degeneres, for example.*

4.   *Read something hilariously funny. What makes you laugh? Who makes you laugh? Erma Bombeck, maybe, or Dave Barry? What funny books have your friends recommended? Pick one up at the library or store and read through it, laughing all the way.*

Remember, after you've brought the riches of laughter into your life, you can work on bringing other flavors of abundance into your sphere. Just like you had the power to create healing laughter by going through the steps listed above, you also have the power to create and attract any other form of riches to you. Abundance, like everything, is a choice—will you choose it for yourself? Of course!

Today's Affirmation: I know which riches are meaningful to me. I can bring them into my life when I desire to. Any time of day or night, I am able to envision myself immersed in the riches which are important to me. I can swim in the warm, soothing energy of abundance in my mind. I know that when I do this, I take one step closer to bringing these riches into my life.

I do not need to wait. Riches are plentiful and varied. I can select one form of riches today and bring it into my life. I am capable. I am resourceful, and I am able to create abundance that brings me joy. I am generous, and I share my abundance with the people in my life. The universe is full of abundance. I am able to tap into this whenever I choose to.

My Personal Thoughts

_____

_____

_____

_____

_____

_____

_____

_____

_____

_____

You are invited to continue the relationship at YourAngelChannel.com

Today's Action Item

Think About It

- Abundance comes in many flavors. In order to bring the riches you want into your life, it pays to spend time thinking about what abundance means to you and which riches you value most.

- When you envision yourself immersed in the riches of your choosing, you begin to align your entire self with the energy, thinking, and feeling needed to bring this form of abundance into your life.

- You have the power to bring some form of riches into your life this very day, and other forms this week. You can then continue steadily along this process, first envisioning your riches and then attracting them to yourself.

7

Affirm Yourself

For the most part, we women are very good at complimenting others. A friend's new dress gets noticed and admired. A child's school artwork receives our warm praise. We flatter our lovers, family members, and friends with our sincere, heartfelt compliments. Where we often need improvement, however, is in affirming ourselves.

And yet, this is one of the most empowering acts we can do for ourselves. It doesn't take much effort, nor does it have to interrupt our daily schedule. We can affirm ourselves anytime, anywhere. We can do so out loud, or we can affirm ourselves discretely in our minds.

Some women feel uncomfortable doing this. We feel it's egotistical or narcissistic, or else we're simply not used to praising ourselves. It's high time we learn to do this, though. It's not about ego, it's about self-respect. It's about giving ourselves the same level of care and respect that we reserve for others. Affirming ourselves raises our self-esteem and reminds us to take care of ourselves, just as we care for others. It's about nurturing our own hearts.

What do you accomplish by affirming yourself? To begin with, you:

- Give yourself a boost along your personal journey

- Help yourself reach your goals

- Shift your thinking to a proactive, can-do pattern

- Give yourself the support you need as you attract your abundance

- Supply yourself with positive feedback to uplift you every step of the way.

According to the universal law of affirmation, "What you say is what you get." In other words, you manifest abundance in your life in part by what you tell yourself. Are you telling yourself that you can, or that you can't? Do you convince yourself that a task is possible or impossible?

Sometimes you may find yourself looking at others and thinking, "She has better luck than me," or perhaps, "People like her better," or maybe even, "Everything always goes well for her." You may compare yourself to this other person and feel jealous or envious. Let me tell you, she has nothing on you. Believe me, you are just as lucky, likable, and competent as she is. The difference is in your perception and perspective.

You are invited to continue the relationship at YourAngelChannel.com

You attract your fortune, your loving people, your success by regarding yourself well, not by downing yourself and being envious of others.

Think about it. You have certain skills and talents that others don't possess. Everybody has something she's good at, no exceptions. Do you not see your own unique gifts, some of which you were born with and others which you've developed over time? Is it because you are blinded by your false perception of lack and less-than?

It's time to make a shift. It's time to change your thinking so that instead of feeling that you are less endowed than others, you start to see and appreciate the wonderful qualities and talents you possess. You are so special! Goodness gracious, you have a lot to offer. Shine like the star you are. The following exercises will help. They'll teach you how to affirm yourself and hold yourself up as highly as you hold your loved ones.

Exercise 1: Embrace Beautiful Words

I want you to get comfortable with paying yourself a compliment. In this two-part exercise, you'll start by complimenting others, something you most likely already do well. Then you'll turn it around and direct praise and compliments back to yourself.

Think about three very special people in your life. They could be friends, family members, mentors, role models, or even people you don't know personally but whom you admire greatly. Think about what you like about these three individuals. What makes them special? What adjectives would you use to describe these wonderful people? Write them down:

What I Like And Appreciate About Person #1:

_____

_____

_____

_____

_____

_____

_____

What I Like And Appreciate About Person #2:

_____

_____

_____

_____

_____

You are invited to continue the relationship at YourAngelChannel.com

_____

_____

_____

_____

What I Like And Appreciate About Person #3:

_____

_____

_____

_____

_____

_____

_____

_____

All right, now clear your mind. Look out the window, or look at a beautiful object, such as a flower vase or painting. Take several deep

You are invited to continue the relationship at YourAngelChannel.com

breaths. When you are ready, look back at the adjectives and descriptions you just wrote down. Do not think about the people they are describing. Focus solely on the words and their meanings.

Read each word silently, then aloud. For each descriptor, stop and reflect on its meaning for a moment. When you've finished reading and reflecting on each one, go back to the start of the list. Now, bring each adjective back to yourself. As you read each out loud, ask yourself, "Does this describe some aspect of who I am?"

No need to rush through. Take your time with each depiction. Can you tie it to yourself somehow? Does it describe a part of you, or some aspect of your life? If yes, circle it. Go through the list and circle every adjective and description that resonates with you.

When you're done, go back and read the list of circled words and descriptions. Direct these beautiful words to yourself. For example, let's say you chose the words "creative, compassionate, and responsible." You can say to yourself, "I am creative, responsible, and compassionate." Say it out loud, with conviction. Repeat it several times. Every time you utter this powerful and true "I am" phrase, feel it down to every cell of your body.

Exercise 2: Empowering Word Search

Attracting abundance into your life involves immersing yourself in all things good and uplifting. For this exercise, you're going to spend a light moment doing something fun—a word search. Not just any word search, though. You'll be looking for some of the most beautiful, loving, and empowering words that exist in our language.

You are invited to continue the relationship at YourAngelChannel.com

The puzzle portion of this exercise, the actual word search, engages your logical mind. The meaning associated with each positive word stirs your emotions. And overall, this exercise uplifts your spirit and elevates your energy levels.

Grab a pencil, sit back, and enjoy this empowering word search. At the bottom of the search you'll find all the beautiful words hidden within this puzzle.

```
R A L Y S C R B M E L D Q Z X P S F G I U V
E N T W E R A D F M O I E O L D E A R L F W
T R A M S O W O V W I W F P K I N D G U A S
C A P A B L E I A M L O R T A M D I W I N A
A M I S O L B O L D I N E I W I M A B Q T S
R L O V I N G I B M R D E N J K A D I O A U
I W J K A N P R I C E L E S S W L O I J S O
N I K M I M O A D O R E D W Y X G I E M T I
G L E M O S E W A B E A U T I F U L I S I C
W O N D E R F U L I T O B E A U T F U M C E
D I G N I F I E D Y E W I L I L I E O N X R
A B C L O V A B L E B E C Z M A W E I W S P
X Y Z W K I W B D Y N A M I C W E R J K S M
D R E M G O L T O B M E I S B L S I N G I T
C A R C R E A T I V E Y E P W O W I L I K E
D O I T F R Y R S L F P O W E R F U L Y O U
S E S D S G B S K A S B C Z T A I S I W I L
V A R M W M A R V E L O U S H P Y I M J T P
P R D C U T I E O V L A N O I T A S N E S I
F L E W T W P Z U C R E A T W W M X J B W J
L A R S B G K S D E A G R A T E F U L S O I
S I W W S P E C T A C U L A R D O O G Y E S
```

Precious	Awesome	Smart	Capable
Beautiful	Caring	Sensational	Creative

You are invited to continue the relationship at <u>YourAngelChannel.com</u>

Lovable	Dynamic	Adored	Powerful
Bold	Loving	Free	Grateful
Dear	Fantastic	Dignified	Marvelous
Wonderful	Spectacular	Kind	Priceless

Exercise 3: Accept Praise With Grace And Gratitude

Think of a person you love and trust. Share with this special person your goal of learning how to accept praise. Ask her or him to give you three compliments. They can be anything of her or his choice, but they must be genuine, and they must be kind.

After your dear one has thought of three compliments to give you, she or he is to say them aloud to you, one by one. For each one that you hear, you are to graciously accept the praise. Say "thank you." When you both are done with this exercise, hug your friend, and thank her or him for helping you affirm yourself.

Doesn't it feel wonderful to be affirmed? Whether it comes from the mouth of another person, or from your own mouth, or from your heart, an affirmation lifts you up. It validates the incredible, powerful being you are. Don't wait for others to compliment you. Affirm yourself on a regular basis. You deserve to shower yourself with kind words and abundant praise.

Today's Affirmation: *I am a marvelous person, dear to others just as they are dear to me. My heart is grateful for the boundless blessings I* *enjoy each day. I know that I am precious to the awesome Creator who lovingly brought me into this existence. Boldly I walk forth, knowing that I am free to make the choices which bring me priceless riches and fantastic abundance.*

Every moment I treat myself kindly. I know I am wonderful, dignified, lovable, adored. I know I am creative, powerful, smart, caring, and capable. My life is beautiful, and I am a dynamic, sensational woman. With a thankful heart I make every moment spectacular!

My Personal Thoughts

_____

_____

_____

_____

_____

_____

_____

_____

_____

You are invited to continue the relationship at YourAngelChannel.com

_____

_____

_____

_____

Today's Action Item

_____

_____

_____

_____

_____

_____

_____

_____

_____

_____

_____

_____

_____

Think About It

- Every moment we have a choice to lift ourselves up. Why not choose to do so right now?

- When we affirm ourselves, we grow in self-respect, self-esteem, self-reliance, and self-love. We show that we are grateful for our qualities and abilities.

- There is no need to wait for others to praise you. Take the time each day to give thanks for who you are and to affirm the uniqueness and special-ness of wonderful, incredible *you*.

Do You Know What You're Attracting?

Perhaps you've never thought of yourself as a magnet, but really, that is what you are—a human magnet. Sounds funny, doesn't it? But in truth, this is what you are. As a human magnet, you attract to yourself so much: people, thoughts, ideas, opportunities, desires, energies. Question is, do you know what you're attracting to yourself? And, do you know how you're doing it?

We attract to ourselves not only through what we say and how we behave, but also through what we think, how we feel, and what kind of energy we emit. Every state of our being is involved when it comes to attracting stuff our way: our emotional state, our mental state, our spiritual state, our physical state. Your entire makeup at this very moment is working to attract many things your way right now.

The Universal Law Of Attraction states, quite simply, that "like attracts like." Such a simple statement, and yet, one that is so misunderstood by many. We may not realize it, but sometimes we want things so badly that we put ourselves in a state of desperation. Since like attracts like, desperation attracts more desperation. Those who think the law doesn't work are incorrect. It's just that they haven't fully understood how it works and how to use it properly.

To attract to yourself the riches and abundance you wish for, you must make sure that you are in a calm and balanced state. Your outlook is positive. Your viewpoint is more optimistic, less pessimistic. It is well in your soul. You are satisfied with yourself and with where you are in life. Start from this state, and you'll see that you'll attract more good things your way—more calm, more balance, more optimism, more satisfaction.

It's quite simple, really. In order to attract the people you want to meet, the experiences you wish to have, and the possessions you seek to enjoy, you must first be the person you want to be. As always, it begins with you. And sometimes, a little shift is all you need.

Perhaps you just need to slow down a bit. If you're trying to do too much all at once, then you're bringing undue stress into your life, and stress attracts more stress. Perhaps you simply need to stop and count your blessings every so often. An attitude of gratitude attracts more gratefulness, and a thankful heart is one that feels light, not heavy.

Or maybe it's time for a concerted effort to be friendlier and more approachable. A smile or a "hello" to someone you pass creates wonderful energy. As you radiate this friendly energy, more comes your way. You may notice others smiling more at you, or perhaps holding the door open for you or letting you have the last parking spot.

Let it begin with you, and see where it goes. To attract good things into your life, make yourself feel whole and deserving of this goodness. Make sure you give out what you wish to receive. Let's begin with an exercise on kindness.

Exercise 1: Attract Kindness

Since like attracts like, there is a simple, beautiful way to attract kindness into your life: Show kindness to others. In this exercise, you'll start a "Kindness Journal." Think of it as a human interaction experiment, if you like. See how powerfully the law of attraction works to bring you abundance.

In this enjoyable two-week project, you'll record both what you give and what you receive. During Week 1, make an effort to show others kindness many times a day. Your kindness can be directed to people, animal, plants, Mother Earth, spirits—any sentient entity. Each day, record these acts of kindness in detail. Here's a sample "Kindness Journal" page:

Day 1: Giving Kindness

1. *Thanked neighbor for bringing me mis-delivered mail.*

2. *Hugged kids before they went to school. Told them how special they are.*

3. *Gave my dog a tummy rub. Told him he's a good dog.*

4. *Called elderly aunt I haven't talked to in a while.*

5. *At grocery store, let person next to me have the last bunch of bananas on shelf.*

6. *Told tree in my backyard how much I appreciate it and how beautiful it is.*

7. *Sent a special blessing to my loved ones who've passed on.*

Continue giving out kindness and recording each act in your journal. Do this for seven days. At the end of the week, read over everything you've done. Feel a special warmth in your heart for the kindness you have sent out into the world.

At the beginning of the second week, continue to show kindness to others, but don't record these deeds. Instead, become an observer. Notice every time that kindness comes your way. Then record each instance in your journal. Your first-day entry for this second week might look something like this:

Day 1: Receiving Kindness

1. *Received drawing from my child with the words "I Love You, Mommy!" written in crayon.*

2. *Neighbor across the street waved at me.*

You are invited to continue the relationship at <u>YourAngelChannel.com</u>

3. *Co-worker complimented a job I did well.*

4. *My dog came by and put his head on my lap when I was sad.*

5. *A shaded spot opened up for me in a crowded parking lot.*

6. *Felt a warm, happy sensation around my heart when thoughts of my departed grandmother entered my mind.*

7. *Received wonderful letter from a friend I hadn't heard from in years.*

Through your journal, you'll see that like does indeed attract like. The more you give, the more you receive in kind.

In this exercise you practiced with kindness. Now, try practicing with something else. Like fun, generosity, smiles, or anything of your choice. What results do you get? Continue your "attraction" experiment by keeping logs of the instances that you receive in kind.

Exercise 2: Fill Your Mind With Good Things

It makes sense that in order to attract good things to yourself, you need to first lay the foundation to receive this goodness. An effective way of establishing this foundation is by exposing yourself to all that's positive. Fill your mind with good things, and you'll start to see that you'll attract *more* of the good things into your life.

Choose "good news" reading. Instead of focusing on the tragic events of the day, go to online news sources that make it a habit to report about good deeds, breakthrough discoveries with positive ramifications to our world, and happy happenings. Give these sites a try:

Good News Network International
http://www.goodnewsnetwork.org/

Good News Broadcast
http://www.goodnewsbroadcast.com/

Happy News
http://www.happynews.com/

Here's another idea. Go to your local library or bookstore and look for inspirational books. They can be funny, or touching, or a bit of both. You choose. The only requirements are that they be uplifting and that they fill your wonderful mind with good things.

Exercise 3: What's Coming Your Way?

In the first exercise you kept a log of all the kindness you give out and receive. In this exercise, you'll spend a day observing everything that comes your way. Jot it all down—the good, the not so good, the mediocre, the spectacular.

As you go about your daily business, keep a pad of paper near you. Spend the day as a detective, observing what comes your way. From the moment you wake up to right before you go to sleep, record

You are invited to continue the relationship at YourAngelChannel.com

everything that enters your life, including feelings, experiences, events, people, conversations, material items, thoughts, ideas, concerns, joys. When you're ready for sleep, put your pad of paper aside, say a few words of thanks for the day, relax, and turn in for the night.

The next day, review what you've written. For each item, ask yourself, "How did I attract this to myself?" Consider your answers carefully. Write down your thoughts. Don't worry about being "right" or "wrong." Just be. Write down your first impressions.

Next, for each item that you wrote, ask yourself, "Do I want this in my life?" Circle the ones you want, and cross out the ones you don't want. Reread the circled items. Focus on these for a few moments. Utter a prayer of thanks for each of these.

Today's Affirmation: I choose to attract abundance to myself. Riches come in many flavors, and at any given moment I can focus on attracting the riches I wish to savor. I have the power to create joy in my life even during challenges and difficult times. I choose to attract the type of abundance that betters me and those around me. I attract laughter, love, stability, balance, goodness, peace, serenity, and prosperity.

I am grateful for the many good things I attract to my life. I know that by being kind, I attract kindness. To attract good friends, I am a good friend to others. When I want more creativity in my life, I am creative. I have the power and the wherewithal to attract the best and the greatest to myself. I can do it.

You are invited to continue the relationship at YourAngelChannel.com

My Personal Thoughts

Today's Action Item

_____

_____

_____

_____

_____

_____

_____

_____

_____

_____

_____

_____

_____

Think About It

- You can attract drama and chaos, or harmony and serenity. It's a simple yet powerful universal law—what you put out comes back to you.

- Be vigilant about what you're attracting to yourself. If you don't like something in your life, make the shift to begin attracting what you do want and need instead.

- Life gives back in kind. Focus on the positive of each day, each event, each situation, and you'll end up attracting more of the good things to you.

Focus Your Attention

Starting a new project is a lot like going on a honeymoon. You feel excited, elated, energetic, and enthused. You can't wait to begin. You have high hopes and big dreams, and you treat your project with great care, giving it special attention. But over time, the newness fades, and with it the excitement, elation, enthusiasm, and all the other special feelings start to fade, too.

You know it doesn't have to be this way. A project that's dear to you doesn't have to lose its special-ness just because it's lost its newness. You can continue to give it the attention it needs, keeping it alive and moving forward. That's how you complete a project. That's how you enact change in your life. That's how you reach a dream. You focus your attention, even when the newness of it all has gone away.

It's like a good marriage. Or a good wine. It takes time for a batch of wine to turn out well. It takes effort to keep a relationship going strong. Both take focus. Attention. Sometimes discipline. But in the end, it's worth it. Because not only have you experienced a wonderful journey and grown along the way, you've also created something beautiful, something worthwhile to you.

Bringing abundance into your life requires focus, because in our modern-day world, it is oh so easy to get distracted. You turn on the television to see what's on. You log on to your computer to see if anyone's emailed you, or to see what's happening in the world. You go to your kitchen to see what you can find to nibble on. Every one of us can too easily spend our entire days wrapped up in these activities!

Then there are the chores we need to get done … the laundry, the cooking, the housecleaning, yard work, errands, bill paying, letter writing, grocery shopping, car maintenance. We can do this round the clock and have no time left for our dreams, our goals, our quest for prosperity and abundance. So we *have* to make the time. We have to make our dreams a priority.

Sure, you need to do your chores. Sure, you need to keep up with current events and friends. And certainly you need to eat. But these activities should not consume your every waking moment, day in and day out. These activities occupy part of your time, but they shouldn't comprise your sole focus. To achieve your abundance, you need to focus your attention there.

This translates into different goals for different women. For some, it may mean going back to school to learn a vocation or earn certain credentials. For others, it may mean making time each day for their passion—writing, art, entrepreneurship, whatever that passion may be. For others still, it could mean investing in the right equipment, or allocating a special space in which to focus energy and attention towards a specific goal.

The means will differ from one woman to the next, but one thing remains in common for all: the need to *focus*. Apply your time, energy, concentration, and attention towards your heart's desire. Discipline yourself to work each day on your goal, whatever it may be. Every day, focus on this a few minutes more. You can do it!

Let's begin by practicing how to focus. The goal of this first exercise is to help you focus exclusively on one task until it's done. With time and with practice, this task becomes easier. It's very important to finish what you start. This exercise will train you to do just that.

Before you begin, I want to share with you this beautiful quote from motivational speaker Anthony Robbins:

> *"It's not what's happening to you now*
> *or what has happened in your past*
> *that determines who you become.*
> *Rather, it's your decisions*
> *about what to focus on,*
> *what things mean to you,*
> *and what you're going to do about them*
> *that will determine your ultimate destiny."*
> – Anthony Robbins

Exercise 1: Practice Focusing

To bring abundance into your life and attract those special riches you want, you need to stay focused. Making changes is a process, not a one-time event. A process is a type of project, isn't it? As with any project, the newness of it will fade. Just make sure the special-ness doesn't fade with it. Protect your efforts by learning how to focus your attention on seeing them to completion. Learn to focus by practicing. Begin with this exercise:

Make a list of five tasks to complete today. While it's true that we women are fantastic multi-taskers, your job here is to place all your attention on one task before moving on. You are not to jump around between tasks. You are to complete them in the order that you wrote them. Work through Task #1 until it's done. Check it off your list. Then move on to Task #2. When it's done, check it off the list. Continue to work your way down the list, until at last Task #5 is done.

Do not give in to distractions. Stay on course as you work through your list. Unless something truly demands your attention, such as a call from your child's school or any other urgent matter, do not give into it. Stick to the five tasks at hand. When you've completed every one, reward yourself with a walk outdoors or a warm cup of herbal tea.

Exercise 2: Rethink Discipline

For many people, discipline is not a very fun word. It evokes images of hardship, toil, even punishment. But did you know that discipline is really a wonderful word? With discipline, we are able to accomplish great things. Effective, loving discipline is *not* about punishment or penalizing others or yourself for mistakes. It's about training. It's about learning. It's about order.

To have discipline, or to be disciplined, means to be able to focus on your goal to the point that you're able to achieve it, and to put aside distractions so you can get there. Think about this for a moment. How would you define the positive aspects of discipline? Write them down:

To me, discipline means…

_____

_____

_____

_____

_____

_____

_____

_____

… and this is a positive thing because…

_____

You are invited to continue the relationship at YourAngelChannel.com

_____

_____

_____

_____

_____

_____

_____

Having discovered this, I plan to make discipline my friend. I will use it to…

_____

_____

_____

_____

_____

_____

_____

_____

_____

Now that you have explored the concept of discipline and re-thought its meaning so that it can serve you better, see if these possible definitions of the word "discipline" resonate with you:

- ✓ *Training, as in training yourself a new system, way of life, or manner of conduct that serves you better*

- ✓ *Control, as in having sufficient self-control to focus on a goal in order to reach it*

- ✓ *Education, as in educating yourself to other ways of behaving, living, or acting in order to further yourself in some manner*

- ✓ *Practice, as in "practice makes perfect"*

- ✓ *Willpower, as in having enough willpower to forfeit immediate gratification in favor of long-term success and fulfillment*

- ✓ *Self-mastery, self-restraint*

Do you see how discipline and focus go hand in hand? Write down your observations:

You are invited to continue the relationship at YourAngelChannel.com

_____

_____

_____

_____

_____

_____

_____

_____

Exercise 3: Practice Refocusing

It's true, sometimes all of us spend too much time focusing on things that aren't good for us. We worry too much. Or we focus our thoughts and energy on situations over which we have little control, in the process working ourselves up into a frenzy.

Tell you what, let's make it a point to stop doing that. Let's try to minimize the time and energy we put into senseless worrying. How do we do this? By refocusing our thoughts.

You are invited to continue the relationship at YourAngelChannel.com

I have here a list of words. On the left side are the "worry" words. On the right side are the associated "freeing" words which come from refocusing your thoughts and your energy. Whenever you find yourself obsessed over one of the worries, find its transformed partner and focus on that instead. Go through the list and give it a try now. Then, keep it handy so that you can refocus on the "better" thought:

Worry Words	Freeing Words
Guilt	Joy
Fear	Love
Should	Can
Danger	Protection
Have To	Want to
Not enough	Plenty
Insufficient	More than enough
Lack	Abundance
Failure	Success
Foolish	Wise
Not qualified	Talented and gifted
Ugly	Beautiful beyond belief
Stupid	Smart—an incredible mind
Poor	Rich in every measure
Restrictions	Liberation, freedom!
Limitations	Opportunities
Unlovable	Loved every moment of every day

You are invited to continue the relationship at YourAngelChannel.com

Words carry a certain energy. Sounds are vibrations, and these vibrations reach us, touch us, and affect us. Instead of letting negative or worry words become the focus of our attention, let's have the freeing words touch our spirits and transform us.

Say these freeing words to yourself over and over again. Repeat them daily for a week. At the end of the week, take stock. Do you notice less worry? More joy? Remember, your focus becomes your reality. Focus on the right words and thoughts, and it will make all the difference for you.

Today's Affirmation: My mind is beautiful. It is a wonderful tool that serves me well. With my mind, I focus on what I need to do, think, feel, believe, and say to attract fantastic abundance to my life. My mind is a tool that I use well and responsibly.

I focus every intent, every emotion, my attention, and all of my energy into that which creates abundance. If something does not serve me well, I gently release it. In its place I bring to me the right people, places, events, thoughts, ideas, projects, efforts, actions, and decisions. I focus on what brings me joy and harmony. I focus my attention on the life-building energy of love.

My Personal Thoughts

_____

_____

_____

_____

_____

_____

_____

_____

_____

_____

_____

_____

Today's Action Item

_____

_____

_____

Think About It

- Whatever you wish to attract, you need to focus your energy, efforts, thoughts, actions, and attention to. If you wish to be a writer, you must write. If you want generosity, you must focus on being a generous individual. If you desire greater joy, then focus your mind, heart, and feelings into that which brings you joy.

You are invited to continue the relationship at YourAngelChannel.com

- Commitment goes hand in hand with focus. First, focus your whole being into achieving the abundance you want. Then, commit yourself to going through the process that will bring that abundance to you.

- Keep your eye on the prize. When distractions try to pull you away from your desired results, gently push them away and refocus your attention to your abundance.

The Time To Act

We can do all the marvelous dreaming and the careful planning in the world, but you and I both know that until we put our ideas into action, nothing really happens. There comes a time when we have to act. It's a simple law of the universe.

In your youth, did you get the chance to spend summer days at a pool or a lake with others your age? Or if there are children in your life now, perhaps you have the chance to spend time watching youngsters enjoying water fun. You might notice that some kids seem to want to jump in, but they're afraid to, and so they stand shivering at the side of the pool for a long, long time (remember the very first time you tried to dive in?). And then there are others who jump right in without even thinking, but then they have to be pulled out by a parent or lifeguard because they're not quite ready to swim yet.

This summertime example can teach you a lot about the right time to take action. It's not good to wait, and wait, and wait some more out of fear, because then you miss out on all the fun. But it's also not good to jump right in if you aren't properly prepared. There is a season and a time for everything—a time to dream, a time to plan, a time to prepare, and a time to act.

What are some of the reasons people are afraid to take action? They include:

- Fear of failing

- Fear of succeeding

- Fear of looking foolish

- Fear of being insufficiently prepared

- Fear of not knowing what to do or how to proceed

- Fear of not having the right training to do it

- Fear of change

- Fear of the unknown

In each case, it's *fear* that holds us back. But fear is not reality. Fear is an emotion, and we actually have more control over our emotions and feelings than we realize. All we need to do is align ourselves with love, and trust in ourselves and in the universe. The fear will lessen and eventually disappear.

So instead of letting fear stop you from taking action, turn things around. Convert that energy of fear into an energy of excitement, joy, anticipation, and ultimately action.

Let's look at each fear again, one at a time, and see how to convert it into something that instead of hindering you will help you:

Fear of failing: When you fail, you learn something very valuable, and that lesson serves you well for your next attempt. Change this to *anticipation for learning important lessons that will help along the journey*.

Fear of succeeding: Success is what you want! There is no reason to fear it. If once you get there you realize it's not what you wanted after all, no problem. You can change your course at any time. But the success you achieve will not be in vain, because it will serve as a springboard to launch you in the direction you wish to go next.

Fear of looking foolish: Who hasn't looked foolish at some point in her life? It's OK, it just means you're human. And there are marvelous, successful people who make a living out of looking foolish, and we love them for it! Look at Lucille Ball, Robin Williams, Whoopi Goldberg. They make us laugh, which is so good for the soul. So looking foolish isn't the end of the world. It's all a matter of perspective.

Fear of being insufficiently prepared: My advice to you is to prepare as best you can, and then go for it. If you fail, no worries.

You are invited to continue the relationship at YourAngelChannel.com

You'll learn something, you'll prepare a bit more, and you'll try again.

Fear of not knowing what to do or how to proceed: Trust your intuition, my dear. It won't let you down. It'll guide you along your way. And don't forget all of your angels and spiritual guides, too. They are there to help and guide you. You are never alone.

Fear of not having the right training to do it: Life experience offers us some of the best training available. You do not need to have a Ph.D. to succeed. If you choose to obtain one, that's great! But if you don't have one, do not feel "less than." You have gifts and talents, skills and life training that will help you in countless scenarios.

Fear of change: Philosophers and sages throughout the ages have stated this in one form or another ... *"The only constant is change."* All things are ever flowing. If there was no change, life would be stagnant, boring. Change is good—embrace it!

Fear of the unknown: It is actually exciting to see what waits around the corner. There is no need to fear that which you don't yet know. Trust in yourself, trust in the process, and enjoy the journey!

In the following exercises, you will learn how to become more comfortable with taking action. You will practice taking action by first doing a little mental preparation and then taking actual steps to get you there. After launching this exciting process, you'll learn how to keep it going and keep it alive. Finally, you'll go the distance. At the end, be prepared to be amazed at what you've accomplished!

You are invited to continue the relationship at YourAngelChannel.com

Exercise 1: Ready, Set, Action!

You have done the groundwork to prepare yourself mentally, emotionally, and spiritually to receive the abundance you desire and deserve. You have done well—congratulate yourself for reaching this point! You have made great progress. The next step is to get comfortable with taking action to bring riches into your life. This exercise will help you do just that—take solid action.

In the previous chapters you've spent time considering what riches you wish to bring into your life. Thinking about these, select one that you'll be working on for this exercise. Write it down:

The particular type of riches I've chosen to work on in this exercise is…

_____

_____

_____

_____

_____

_____

_____

_____

_____

    Spend a few moments pondering why you'd like to bring these riches into your life at this time. Write down your reasons:

I've chosen to bring these riches into my life at this time because...

_____

_____

_____

_____

_____

_____

_____

    Next, think about the ways in which you'll benefit, and write these down.

Through these riches, I'll be able to enjoy these benefits:

You are invited to continue the relationship at YourAngelChannel.com

_____

_____

_____

_____

_____

_____

_____

_____

_____

Perfect, you've successfully brought these riches into your personal realm of possibilities. Now take the next step. Take action to bring this particular flavor of abundance into your life. Come up with five steps that you'll be taking to bring these riches to you. Perhaps they're the first five steps, or perhaps they're five of the more major steps, or maybe they encompass the entire process from start to finish. You choose. Write them down:

Step 1:

_____

_____

_____

_____

_____

_____

_____

_____

_____

Step 2:

_____

_____

_____

_____

_____

_____

_____

_____

Step 3:

_____

_____

_____

_____

_____

_____

_____

_____

Step 4:

_____

_____

_____

You are invited to continue the relationship at YourAngelChannel.com

_____

_____

_____

_____

_____

Step 5:

_____

_____

_____

_____

_____

_____

_____

_____

All right, you are now ready to take the exciting leap. Work on Step 1. Jump right in, and get as much of Step 1 done as you can today. At the end of the day, look back at what you've accomplished. Congratulate yourself for your courage and your initiative. You have empowered yourself by launching the process to bring to you the riches that you want. Hurray!

Exercise 2: Keep Going!

Continue to work on Step 1 from the first exercise until you've completed it. When you're done, begin Step 2. Work on it until it's done. Continue down the list until you've completed all five steps in their entirety.

You may find it helpful to keep a log as you go. In this log list everything that's going smoothly, the challenges and obstacles you encounter, how you resolve issues, and what to do next time to simplify or speed up the process. Also write down how these riches are starting to manifest in your life.

Be patient with the process. Trust the process. Continue forward, taking action and working on your goals a little at a time. On the days that you have more energy and time to devote to your steps, go for it! On days that you have less time and energy, make sure to devote at least some of yourself to your goal anyways. The important thing is that you keep moving forward towards your goal until you reach it.

Exercise 3: Go The Distance

You have now completed five steps towards attracting abundance to yourself. How do you feel? Don't be surprised if you feel energized, empowered, enriched, and with an elevated sense of confidence!

Now that you've completed these steps, take the time to evaluate where you are. Is there more left to do? Are there additional steps you can take to complete the process of bringing these specific riches of your choice into your life? If so, what are these steps? Write them down:

Additional Steps:

_____

_____

_____

_____

_____

_____

_____

_____

_____

You are invited to continue the relationship at YourAngelChannel.com

_____

_____

_____

_____

Begin working on the next step today. As in the previous exercise, continue working on it until it's done, then move to the next step. Or it's possible that you can take shortcuts and combine certain steps, working on them in parallel. Feel free to do so—you are now an advanced action-taker, so mix and match steps as needed to fulfill your personal abundance.

When you've completed the process, stand back once more and look at your accomplishments. Be proud of yourself and what you've done. Take particular note of how you've grown in the process. With greater abundance comes personal growth. What a winning combination!

Today's Affirmation: I have dreamed magnificent dreams. I have envisioned myself swimming in a sea of abundance. I am ready for the next step. I am ready to take action in accordance with the riches I wish to bring to myself.

The time has come to merge intent with action. I align my actions with my desires, and I am excited by the results I am achieving and will continue to achieve. I am so happy to empower myself by taking constructive, positive action. I dream of riches, and I take action to make these dreams my reality.

My Personal Thoughts

_____

_____

_____

_____

_____

_____

_____

_____

_____

_____

_____

Today's Action Item

Think About It

- We realize our dreams by first aligning ourselves with our deepest desires and then taking effective, consistent action to see our dreams through.

- Every success story, every achiever, every woman who has attained the abundance she desires has taken action to reach her personal riches.

- Taking action advances you forward and leads to the results you want, giving you a wonderful sense of accomplishment and achievement.

11

Believe In Yourself

All types of people have come into your life. Many of them have believed in you. Perhaps your parents or guardians taught you that you are special. Perhaps a cherished grandparent, aunt, or uncle showed you that you can reach for the stars. You may have been fortunate to have mentors or special people watching over you and teaching you how to reach your potential—teachers, counselors, ministers, coaches, librarians, friends. If you had people such as these teaching you to believe in yourself, you are very fortunate, indeed.

Even with others believing in you, there comes a point when YOU have to believe in yourself. Just as there came a time when you had to walk on your own, without holding the hand of a trusted grownup, and you had to ride your bike on your own, without the security of those training wheels, there comes a time in your life when you have to believe in who you are, by yourself. You cannot rely on the compliments and accolades from others. Surely these are nice. They boost your self-esteem and make you feel good. They show that others value you. But ultimately you have to stand on your own two feet and validate yourself.

There are many reasons for this. First of all, others can encourage and uplift you, but they can't build your self-esteem for you. This lies within your own power. There are some very talented people out there, but because they don't believe in themselves, they are held back from reaching their full potential. I don't want this to happen to you.

People who believe in themselves are neither egotistical nor narcissistic. Simply, they are grateful and realistic. They are thankful for the talents they were born with, the talents they acquired, and the fortitude within themselves. And they realize that in order to access their abundance, they are free to use everything at their disposal—every ability and skill they possess. Believing that they CAN do it helps them to achieve their prosperity.

Maybe you've had people in your life who believed in you, and maybe you haven't had anybody yet recognize your beauty, your special-ness, your uniqueness. Maybe there have been people in the past who've believed in you, but nobody seems to acknowledge your gifts today. Please do not be discouraged. Understand that YOU can uplift yourself anytime. You can't control what others think or say, but you can take charge and give yourself the validation you so richly deserve.

In the following exercises, you'll be doing just that: Learning how to validate yourself, anywhere, anytime, and boosting yourself so that you can believe in wonderful YOU with all your might!

You are invited to continue the relationship at YourAngelChannel.com

Exercise 1: Positive Self-Talk To Your Reflection

Take a look in the mirror. Look at yourself as though you were looking at another person, specifically, at a dear friend. Refrain from being critical. Instead, look at yourself in a compassionate, nonjudgmental way. See yourself as a wonderful creation, a magnificent being, a spiritual child of God/Goddess. See yourself for who you truly are.

Smile at the beautiful reflection in the mirror looking back at you. Regardless of your appearance, you are beautiful, just the way you are. Find one thing that you like about the way you look—the glow of your skin, the radiance in your eyes, the way your hair crowns your head, your cheery clothes, anything you find pleasing. Out loud, give yourself a compliment regarding this magnificent aspect of yourself.

Next think about one of your many special qualities, perhaps your resolve, your ability to empathize with others, the way you listen to a friend in need, how you stick up for someone being mistreated, or anything else you wish to focus on. Once you've chosen one of your qualities, reflect upon it for a few moments. Then, out loud, compliment this aspect of yourself.

Continue to gaze at your reflection. See the fabulous woman you are. Say out loud,

"I am special. I am a vital part of this planet. I am able to contribute to Mother Earth's magnificent existence. In turn, I am able to enjoy all the abundance that Earth and the universe have to offer."

You are invited to continue the relationship at YourAngelChannel.com

When you are done, give yourself another big smile and envision yourself being bathed in a beautiful, warm glowing light. Close your eyes and picture yourself as part of a giant network of strong, caring women. See yourself and your sisters circling the globe. Envision yourself and every other woman spreading the same warm glow that envelops you now around Mother Earth. Feel the healing effect of this energy on you, your fellow sisters, and your beautiful home, Earth.

Open your eyes. Looking at your reflection, repeat these words out loud,

"I give and accept healing. I give and accept love. I give and accept abundance. Let it be."

Exercise 2: Give Yourself A Gift

Before you can accept the bounty that the universe has to offer, you have to learn how to graciously receive a gift. What a perfect time to do so. You have worked diligently, reaching this point in the book and in your progression. Congratulate yourself! And reward yourself with a small but meaningful gift.

The nature of this gift is entirely of your choice. I will merely provide some ideas here to get you thinking. You may pick something from this list, or you may come up with your own gift idea. The main thing is to give yourself a present and to feel your worth, your value, and your appreciation as you receive it.

Feel the joy it brings you. Whenever the universe brings you a gift, by whichever means it chooses to, be thankful. Don't say "no thank you" and watch the gift disappear. Take it, give thanks, and enjoy!

List of possible gifts to give yourself:

1. *An hour to yourself to do whatever you enjoy*

2. *A walk through beautiful surroundings*

3. *A refreshing beverage, such as a latte, fruit smoothie, or chai tea from one of your favorite coffeehouses or juice stops*

4. *A book you've been wanting to read for a long time*

5. *An evening with a favorite movie and some popcorn*

6. *A long, luxurious bubble bath*

7. *A new haircut*

8. *Tickets to a theatrical or musical production*

9. *A phone call to a dear friend*

10. *A meal at one of your favorite restaurants*

11. *An ice cream cone, or a serving of your favorite dessert*

12. *A flower bouquet*

You are invited to continue the relationship at YourAngelChannel.com

Exercise 3: You're The Star!

All right, it's time to get your creative juices flowing! For this exercise, you will create something where YOU are the star. You will use your creativity to give yourself honor and worth. Again, the choice is yours, but here are ideas to get you thinking. Use one of them, or come up with your own way to pay tribute to yourself:

1. *Write a story where you are the heroine.*

2. *Create a beautiful poem about yourself—what makes you fantastic?*

3. *Draw or paint a picture that reflects something wonderful about you.*

4. *Create a new recipe that celebrates you!*

5. *Using old magazines, make a collage about you and some of your favorite things.*

Today's Affirmation: I am a confident woman. I know in my heart of hearts that I am capable of reaching my abundance. I am worthy of bountiful riches in my days and nights. I believe in my self-worth and I know that I am worthy of receiving all the gifts the universe offers me. I am open to receive.

I give myself permission to receive all the goodness that comes my way. I am grateful for these blessings, and I fully accept their presence in my life. With joy and wonder I believe that these gifts come my way for a good reason. I am thankful. I believe.

You are invited to continue the relationship at YourAngelChannel.com

My Personal Thoughts

_____

_____

_____

_____

_____

_____

_____

_____

_____

_____

_____

_____

Today's Action Item

_____

_____

_____

_____

_____

_____

_____

_____

_____

_____

_____

Think About It

- By believing in yourself, you boost your confidence, enabling you to pass through barriers, both real and imagined.

- When we feel worthy, valuable, and important enough to receive good things, we *enjoy* the rewards that we work to achieve.

- You are a marvelous person, a beautiful woman, and a courageous spiritual being, just the way you are. Accept this, and believe in yourself.

12

The Dance Of Giving & Receiving

The energy we send out from our hearts through an act of kindness spreads love everywhere. It returns to us as a form of abundance, perhaps when we least expect it. This abundance may come as an extra hug from our spouse or our child, a hummingbird stopping to greet us, a beautiful rainbow, a loving letter from a dear one far away.

And so we enthusiastically join the universal dance of giving and receiving, because when we give, we receive so much, and when we receive, we are motivated to give more. Daily acts of kindness will come back to us in magnificent ways. Plus, it feels great to help others. The feeling we get is out of this world!

I'd like you to ponder the following thoughts for a moment:

✓ Give freely—a smile, a kind word, free professional advice, a back rub to your spouse—and see how abundantly you receive

✓ Give with an open heart and a cheerful outlook, and receive in the same spirit

✓ The energy you release is the same energy that returns to you

✓ Be open to receiving, and you'll have more to give

✓ The more you give, the more you are able to receive

What do you think about each of the preceding statements? Which ones ring true for you? Why? How would you rephrase each in your own words? How might changes happen in your life if you were to internalize one or more of these statements and make it your truth? How might this help you achieve your abundance?

After you've had enough time to consider these questions, try the following exercises. As always, proceed at your own pace. Take the time you need to complete each to your satisfaction. And of course, have fun with them.

Exercise 1: Give This Day In Five Ways

Every single day we are presented with a plethora of opportunities to give generously and to receive graciously. When we give and receive, there is a flow of energy involve, and this flow is as essential to us as the very breath we take in and release. It helps us to feel alive.

There are countless ways to give. You can give of your time, your energy, your caring, your involvement, your finances, your love, your attention, your special talent, your thoughts and prayers. Now, come up with five ways that you can gave on this day. If it's early in the day, you can give these five special gifts today. If it's late at night, then plan to give these tomorrow. Or, spread them out over the week, doing one a day.

Write down your five specific ways that you will give of yourself:

Way #1:

_____

_____

_____

_____

_____

You are invited to continue the relationship at YourAngelChannel.com

_____

_____

_____

Way #2:

_____

_____

_____

_____

_____

_____

_____

_____

Way #3:

_____

You are invited to continue the relationship at YourAngelChannel.com

_____

_____

_____

_____

_____

_____

_____

_____

Way #4:

_____

_____

_____

_____

_____

_____

_____

You are invited to continue the relationship at YourAngelChannel.com

_____

_____

Way #5:

_____

_____

_____

_____

_____

_____

_____

_____

   Now that you've written them down, go out into the world and, in your own way, deliver these five gifts. Again, if it's morning or early afternoon, you can complete this exercise today. If it's late, then complete this activity tomorrow. If you prefer, take a week to deliver your special gifts.

When you finish, take a moment to reflect on how giving makes you feel. What do you feel inside? Write it down:

Today I gave, and now I feel...

_____

_____

_____

_____

_____

_____

_____

_____

Exercise 2: Feel Worthy To Receive

As we covered in the previous chapter, you are very worthy of receiving magnificent gifts! The universe wishes to bestow good things upon you. Accept them. Practice how to trust that the universe delivers, and practice feeling worthy of this bounty:

You are invited to continue the relationship at YourAngelChannel.com

1. *If the weather is nice, go outdoors. Feel the sunshine warm you up. Feel the breeze on your face. Look around—notice the beauty of your surroundings. Look at the beautiful sky. Look at the signs of nature around you. These are gifts for you, completely free for the taking. Take a moment to enjoy and appreciate them.*

2. *If the weather doesn't lend itself to being outdoors, then look out your favorite window. What do you see? Is there a storm raging outside? A snow blizzard? A gentle rainfall? Isn't it exciting to watch nature in action? This, too, is a gift for you. Enjoy it.*

3. *Bite into a delicious fruit. Notice its juiciness, its texture, its unique flavor. Take another bite, and another. Enjoy the experience.*

4. *Take in the aroma of a flower. Notice how wonderful it makes you feel inside. What precious memories does the aroma evoke? This, too, is a gift for you.*

5. *Select a piece of music that you enjoy, and take a moment to listen to it. Hear the notes rise and fall, the tempo speed up and slow down, creating a magnificent symphonic experience for you. Enjoy how the harmonious sounds make you feel.*

These are all wonderful gifts for you! They are given to you each day. These and many, many more gifts. Acknowledge them. Appreciate them. Enjoy them all!

You are invited to continue the relationship at YourAngelChannel.com

Exercise 3: Give And Receive

You have practiced giving of yourself in five different ways. You also have given yourself permission to receive the abundance the universe wishes to bestow upon you. Now, join in the giving and receiving dance fully. Become a master in this beautiful cosmic flow that connects us all.

Think of someone who has a specific need. Some ideas to get you started:

- *A lonely octogenarian living in a nursing home who could use some company*

- *A child you know struggling with a learning disability*

- *A harried parent who can use a helping hand*

- *A local charity that needs volunteers for a one-time event*

- *Someone at work who's struggling to keep up with her workload*

- *A person who's done something against her value system and needs reassurance that she's still a precious child of God*

- *A friend who's strapped for cash*

- *Someone grieving a major loss*

You are invited to continue the relationship at YourAngelChannel.com

- *An injured person who could use a little temporary help with cooking or housekeeping*

These are examples, but they'll help you think of the real people in your life who have genuine needs. Once you've thought of a person with a need whom you'd like to help, figure out a way to give her or him something that will be of service. Then, offer your help to this person (or group, or charity). Give of yourself in the best way you see fit.

Later on, give yourself a gift. Receive from the abundance that surrounds you and flows freely. Choose which particular gift you want to receive. Ideas include:

- *A leisurely evening of movies and popcorn in the comfort of your home*

- *An afternoon of catching up with a friend*

- *A new book to read, which you can either purchase or pick up at the library*

- *A vibrant bouquet of flowers for yourself, from your garden or from the local florist*

- *A delicious bowl of strawberries, raspberries, or your favorite fruit*

- *An hour of therapeutic massage*

- *A night out listening to concert music or a favorite band*

You are invited to continue the relationship at YourAngelChannel.com

What gift do you wish to receive? Take your pick. It is good to give and receive. Enjoy the abundance that comes from giving of yourself to help others, and also that comes from giving to yourself, because you deserve it. We all do.

Today's Affirmation: I ask, and it is given to me. I seek, and I find. I knock, and the door opens for me. The universe is ever-flowing, involved in an intricate, sacred dance of give and take. I give, and the universe accepts. In turn, I accept all that the universe gives me. We are in a benevolent partnership, supplying one another with what we need.

Every day I choose to give and receive freely. I smile at others, and I accept their smiles. I send kind, gentle thoughts into the world, and I receive kindness and gentleness. My heart is open. It gives abundance and receives abundance. I am richly blessed, and I am thankful.

My Personal Thoughts

_____

_____

_____

_____

_____

_____

You are invited to continue the relationship at YourAngelChannel.com

_____

_____

_____

_____

_____

_____

_____

Today's Action Item

_____

_____

_____

_____

_____

_____

_____

_____

_____

Think About It

- When you're plugged into the dance of freely giving and freely receiving, you experience an aliveness that sparkles and shines.

- Do not give grudgingly, and do not be coerced into giving. Give only from your heart and through your free will.

- Likewise, receive good gifts with a grateful heart and enjoy them to the fullest.

13

Always Give Thanks

When I was much younger, my angel told me to watch the birds. He explained to me that even before the birds look for food, they begin singing a song of thanks. They sing because they are happy knowing that God will provide them with all they need. Isn't this a beautiful concept? What if we lived this way, with a sense of gratitude each day? What a wonderful way to start our mornings.

I believe we should do as these precious little birds do. Let us rise each morning and sing a song of thanks knowing that God is taking care of us and bringing all of us our abundance. Try this—use the letters in the word NOW to help bring abundance to you. N-O-W stands for Notice Only Wonderful abundant things in your life. Do this, and you'll foster a grateful heart which will help you attract more of these wonderful, abundant things!

Regardless of who you are, regardless of what you've been through in your life, regardless of the hardships you've experienced, you truly have much to be grateful for at this very moment. For one thing, you're alive! That means that you've survived. Not only that, but at many levels you are thriving.

You are here on this planet not by accident. You chose to be here, and you were chosen to be here at this place and time. You are here to learn important lessons and to enjoy life abundantly. Believe me when I say that you are a courageous woman with great dignity. Even when you suffer, you exhibit resilience and march forward with hope and resolve. That, too, is something to be thankful for.

I could write an entire book on this topic alone! But perhaps one question is, *why* give thanks? Why is it so important to be grateful? Quite simply, because it's good for your body, mind, and soul. When you appreciate the wonders in your life, as well as the lessons and the gifts, the challenges and the joys, you increase your optimism. You generate more positive emotions, and you increase both your vitality and your satisfaction level. All these are very good for you.

Being thankful gives you power. It enables you to:

- Have a healthy level of respect for yourself – your body, your mind, your self, your personality, your heart, your spirit. This increases your desire to take good care of wonderful you.

- Feel a sense of delight for the people around you, the people you encounter at work, at the store, in your neighborhood, everywhere

- Better manage stress in your life and cope with daily problems

- Have an optimistic outlook

- Boost your immune system

- See beauty and grace even where others may miss it

An attitude of gratitude is a very healthy viewpoint to adopt. It just makes life sweeter, and that's worth it, isn't it? The following exercises will help you to grow in gratitude and to be thankful every day.

Exercise 1: Tour Of Thanks

Walk throughout your house, room by room. Go slowly and purposefully scan each room, looking at various objects throughout, from the walls to the shelves and everywhere else. As you scan each room, pause at the items that carry special meaning for you.

For example, you might notice an item that was a special gift to you from someone you love. A souvenir that you brought back from a trip you thoroughly enjoyed. A handmade memento from a cherished relative. An object that takes you back to an especially significant period from your past. Maybe even something you bought on a whim just because you liked it.

As you take note of all of these special items, enjoy the positive feelings they evoke in you. For each object, pause a moment and utter a little prayer of thanks that this particular item is in your possession. Give thanks for the beautiful memories it brings back.

Tour several rooms of your house and continue your ritual of remembering and of giving thanks. If you like, tour your entire house, including the outside. Give thanks for these very special items you are privileged to have and enjoy.

Exercise 2: People, Places, & More

Throughout our lives, we encounter wonderful people who touch us in a special way. After meeting them, we are transformed, and our spirits are elevated. These individuals help us advance along our spiritual journey. And whether they're in our lives mere moments or many, many years, a part of them remains with us always.

The first thing you'll do in this exercise is list the people and special animal friends who've changed your life and helped you grow. You can write down their names, their initials, or a description—for example, "the teacher's helper in kindergarten who taught me how to tie my shoes." List everyone you're thankful for being a part of your life, whether in the past or the present:

These are the people I wish to express my gratitude for at this time:

_____

_____

_____

_____

_____

_____

_____

_____

_____

Next, think about all the places you've been to. Everything from your lovely backyard to a place far away. Places where you've met wonderful people, learned new things, made discoveries about yourself and the world around you. Make a list of all these special places, and feel free to jot down a couple of words about why they matter to you:

These are the places I have been to that I'm grateful for having discovered:

_____

_____

_____

_____

_____

You are invited to continue the relationship at YourAngelChannel.com

_____

_____

_____

_____

You've listed people and places you're grateful for. Now, I leave it completely up to you. Think of additional things for which you're thankful—ideas, experiences, dreams, achievements, anything. List those next:

I am also thankful for these:

_____

_____

_____

_____

_____

_____

_____

You are invited to continue the relationship at YourAngelChannel.com

Exercise 3: Offer Your Prayer Of Gratitude

Go back to the lists you made in Exercise 2. Read them over, and for each name and each item listed, offer a prayer of thanks, in your own way, in your own words. As you offer your special prayer for each one, feel the gratitude right down to every cell of your body.

Today's Affirmation: I am so thankful for everything in my life. The fun, light moments bring me joy and pleasure. The challenges make me grow. Both are good. I am grateful for every person in my life. Each one teaches me an important lesson that helps me grow in magnificent ways, as a woman, as a person, as a spiritual being on an exciting, endless journey.

Life is a gift, and I am thankful to be here at this moment in time. I am exactly where I need to be. I am living, and learning, and evolving, and every step of the way I am grateful for choosing and for being chosen. I was chosen to be here, and I chose to be here. Life is good. Life is amazing!

My Personal Thoughts

_____

_____

_____

_____

_____

_____

_____

_____

_____

_____

Today's Action Item

_____

_____

_____

_____

_____

_____

_____

_____

_____

_____

_____

_____

_____

Think About It

- Being thankful for the little things in our lives is just as important as being grateful for the big events and achievements.

- Having an attitude of genuine gratitude gives us a boost and propels us forward on our journey.

You are invited to continue the relationship at YourAngelChannel.com

- Saying "thank you" for what you have, for who you are, for the people and pets in your life, and for the events that unfold is one of the purest forms of prayer, undoubtedly picked up by the universe and heard by your God.

14

Don't Quit Now!

Congratulations, you've come this far! In the process you've learned a great deal about yourself and about the wonderful mechanism of reaching your abundance. You've learned how to start shifting your thoughts so that you can begin to think your way to abundance. You've pinpointed changes you'd like to make.

You've practiced envisioning your abundance and prosperity. You've learned to pay attention to what you're attracting, to focus your attention and your efforts, and to validate yourself. You've taken action, given thanks, and learned to better appreciate both giving and receiving. So what's left? Persistence!

It's what some people like to call "stick-to-itness." When you start a new process, as you have done through the exercises and guidance from this book, you have to first of all trust in the process, and you have to also give it enough time to work. It's like anything in life. When you're baking a cake, you can't take it out of the oven before it's done, because it won't work. Instead of fluffy cake you get a gooey mess.

When you first learned to drive, you proceeded systematically, one step at a time—you didn't rush into freeway traffic. But you didn't give up, either; you stuck with it, and eventually you reached the point where you could get on and off that freeway without any difficulties.

It is the same with this exciting process you've launched. You are transforming yourself so that you can attract, attain, and enjoy your abundance. And you're doing this a step at a time, at your own pace. You're doing this in the manner that's most comfortable for you. Trust that you are moving forward. Do not compare your progress with someone else's. You are where you need to be right now, and you will continue to get to where you are going, a step at a time. The important thing is that you keep going. Don't give up! Keep going. Keep moving forward. Little by little, you will reach your goals.

The secret to persistence is that it *always* yields results. Stay with it long enough, and at least some aspect of it will work for you. How does a person build her own successful business? How does an author complete a book? How does a mother build a strong relationship with her children? How does a legislator get a law changed? How does a student earn a college degree? How does an astronaut get to do a spacewalk? All of these take time, educating oneself, working hard, and of course, persistence.

I've stated before that abundance is not something you have to earn … it is your birthright, and you have every right to claim it. For many women and men, the problem is that once they hit that first little bump, or the second or third one, they become so frustrated that they give up. They get discouraged and feel it's just too hard to claim that abundance they so desire.

Yes, there will be some challenges along the way, but you know what? These challenges strengthen us! They help us to grow in numerous, wonderful ways. They stretch us, and in the process we grow in strength, grace, knowledge, wisdom, and confidence.

So please don't let the challenges stop you from claiming what is rightfully yours. Keep this simple yet powerful formula in mind as you proceed:

BE PERSISTENT → GET RESULTS!

Look at other meanings of persistence:

- Perseverance

- Tenacity

- Determination

- Firmness

- Resoluteness

- Resolve

- Doggedness

You are invited to continue the relationship at YourAngelChannel.com

- Endurance

In other words, *Don't Give Up*. Keep going. Keep trying. Keep innovating and creating. The day will come when all your efforts and your persistence will lead to the most glorious results you've envisioned. Isn't that day worth working for? I say yes!

Focus on your goal, continue to make progress every day, but remember this, too: Enjoy the journey. Because the journey, the process, is just as marvelous and rewarding as the destination. In the next exercises, you'll practice persistence and learn the value of sticking to something while doing activities that you enjoy.

Exercise 1: Choose An Activity

Our lives become so busy that we often put aside the very things we love to do. Look at the following list; which of these activities, if any, do you enjoy? Circle or check all the ones that apply:

- *Writing letters*

- *Scrap-booking or creating photo albums*

- *Walking, jogging, or cycling*

- *Traveling*

- *Baking, cooking*

- *Any kind of needlework—sewing, knitting, crochet, embroidery, others*

- *Painting*

- *Creating with your hands—sculpture, pottery, metalwork, woodwork, others*

- *Creative writing—poetry, short stories, plays, others*

- *Dancing, or any other physical activity such as tennis, golf, bowling, team sports*

- *Doing yoga or meditation*

- *Gardening (vegetables, flowers, herbs, other) or landscaping*

- *A musical pursuit—singing, playing an instrument, listening to your favorite style of music*

- *Volunteering, tutoring, mentoring*

- *Taking special interest classes*

- *Practicing a second language*

- *Other Activity:*_____

_____

_____

You are invited to continue the relationship at YourAngelChannel.com

_____

_____

Of the activities that you checked, when is the last time you actually did them? When were you last involved with these activities that you're passionate about, that bring you a tremendous sense of enjoyment and satisfaction?

If it's been a while (such as several months or more), then it's time to get back to doing what you love to do. Pick one of the activities you selected, and make a commitment to doing that activity. Once you're ready, move on to the next exercise.

Exercise 2: Get Into The Process

All right, you've made your selection. Whether it be baking or jogging or tutoring or anything else of your choice, you are now going to make a "commitment plan." Commit to working on this activity each week for a particular length of time.

For example, say you chose "creating photo albums." In your commitment plan, you will list several specifics, such as:

Week 1: Gather up all the photos that have been collecting in boxes over the years.

Week 2: Sort through the photos, selecting which ones to display in an album, and organizing them by date (such as "Summer of 2003").

Week 3: Browse through shops and select a nice photo album.

Week 4: Complete first half of the album.

Week 5: Complete second half of the album.

Be sure to create realistic goals. In the example above, you can extend it to ten weeks instead of five if you know that you're going to be busy with other things. It doesn't really matter how long it takes you to complete your chosen activity. The main thing is that you stick to it. You are practicing persistence.

Here's another example. Say you chose swimming. Your commitment plan might look something like this:

Week 1: Find out where I can swim in my community (pools, lakes, beaches)

Week 2: Visit some of these places and gather information, such as hours of operation, fees, discounts, and so on.

Week 3: Choose a place, day (or days) of the week, and time to swim, and go for your first swim.

You are invited to continue the relationship at YourAngelChannel.com

Weeks 4 – 12: Continue to swim each week.

Of course, once you start an activity such as swimming, you can continue doing it indefinitely. But give yourself a start and end point for the sake of completing this exercise.

Exercise 3: Get It Done

In this next exercise, you're going to go the distance. After you start executing your commitment plan, you may find that you need to make an adjustment here and there. Maybe you have to miss a week. Or perhaps the activity takes you longer than anticipated. Or you're enjoying it so much that you want to expand it, adding additional steps to your original plan. That's OK! As they say, "go with the flow." If you feel moved to make changes or go in a slightly different direction, go for it.

The main thing is to complete your plan. Get it done. Even if it takes you five times as long as you had originally expected. Because when you get it done, you get to enjoy the results.

After you've completed everything listed on your commitment plan, reflect for a moment on where you are. What have you gained? How have you grown? What results have you achieved? Write them down:

These are the results of my efforts:

You are invited to continue the relationship at YourAngelChannel.com

_____

_____

_____

_____

_____

_____

_____

_____

_____

_____

_____

_____

Which of these results are you especially pleased with? Go ahead and circle those. What discoveries have you made about yourself in the process of being persistent?

You are invited to continue the relationship at <u>YourAngelChannel.com</u>

Today's Affirmation: Day by day, step by step, moment after moment, I come closer to my destination. Little by little, I bring abundance into my life. Before I know it, I am swimming in a great, nurturing sea of abundance. I breathe it in, I feel it, I am energized by the abundance that fills every space of my life.

With hope and persistence, I keep moving forward, confident in the success I am bound to achieve. I will not give up, because I know that quitting now would be no fun. I would miss out on what I have worked attentively to achieve. So I keep going, embracing joy, confidence, and courage as my friends. I will succeed. I am succeeding this very moment. I am living in a state of abundance. The universe gives generously, and I accept graciously. I am thankful. I am happy. I am.

My Personal Thoughts

_____

_____

_____

_____

_____

_____

You are invited to continue the relationship at YourAngelChannel.com

_____

_____

_____

_____

_____

_____

_____

Today's Action Item

_____

_____

_____

_____

_____

_____

You are invited to continue the relationship at YourAngelChannel.com

_____

_____

_____

_____

_____

_____

_____

_____

Think About It

- Life is a process, and within this process we launch and pursue many other individual processes, each one teaching us a valuable lesson and bringing us its own reward.

- Whatever is worthwhile merits your time, energy, and commitment. Very little is accomplished overnight. Changes, growth, and lasting transformation all happen over time.

- Reaching your abundance is a very rewarding process. Stick with it, and you'll enjoy bountiful gifts.

15

Giving Back

Every one of us has so much to be thankful for. One way to express our gratitude in a tangible, powerful way is to give back. We know there are many needs out there. We hear about it through the news outlets. We hear it from our friends. We see it in our communities. Each one of us can't possibly solve everything, but if all of us pitch in somehow, contributing in our own unique ways, collectively the difference we make is astounding.

There is no such thing as a small gesture of kindness. Anything you do from your heart makes a big difference. When you help another person, or a cause, or the animal kingdom, or Mother Earth, your act of compassion and kindness lifts up the one you're helping and *you*. Add up all of these acts, and you'll start to see that they elevate humanity and our entire planet to a higher spiritual dimension.

This is happening right now, all around the world, and YOU are a part of it! Doesn't it feel wonderful to be making a difference? Every smile you give to another human being, every compliment, every kind word makes a difference. Every time you give someone a helping hand—tying a child's shoes, opening the door for someone whose hands are full, being there for a friend in need. None of these acts of compassion are ever in vain. They do far more than we may ever realize to create a better world, one kind act at a time.

There are countless ways you can be of service to others. How will you choose to serve your fellow woman and fellow man? How will you bridge generations and make connections? Here are some ideas to get you thinking:

- Read a storybook to a child

- Read stories of inspiration to a nursing home resident

- Cook a meal for someone in need, such as a family with a newborn

- Help build a home for someone in your community (perhaps through an organization such as Habitat for Humanity)

- Volunteer at a kitchen that serves meals to the homeless

- Help at a nearby school or public library

- Write down a few words of inspiration and send them to someone you know who is hurting in some way

You are invited to continue the relationship at YourAngelChannel.com

- Deliver groceries to a shut-in

- Tutor a young person in a subject you know well

- Volunteer at your house of worship or community center

- Share your expertise with others

I'd like to share with you a few ways in which women are giving back through service. Their examples may inspire in you new ideas to create your own way to give back:

- Here's to Madonna Coffman, a retired cardiac nurse who spearheaded the "Locks Of Love" initiative. This nonprofit organization accepts human hair from donors and turns it into wigs for children who've lost their hair due to medical conditions. And kudos to everyone who donates their hair to this worthy cause!

- Here's to Sally Lincoln, a portrait artist who donates her time, energy, and talent by going to the Veteran's Administration Nursing Home and Care Unit in Denver and painting portraits of the residents and patients there. She doesn't charge for her service, her reward being the smiles on the nursing home patients and the sense of dignity her beautiful art gives them.

- Here's to Colleen Steele, an elementary school art teacher in Missouri who donated one of her kidneys so that a former student, Samantha, could live.

You are invited to continue the relationship at YourAngelChannel.com

When you give from your heart, as these ladies do, God gives back to you. To attract money into your life, first use what you have to make God's world a better place. Whatever you give comes back to you in abundance. If you give out positive thoughts and love, you will get back the same.

Of course it's also true that when you put forth negative thoughts, they will return to you. So there is great truth in the adage that "what you give is what you get." There is also truth in that what you do to help others also helps you. We truly are one humanity, and everything you do for another person you also do for yourself. There is a mutual benefit in every act of kindness.

You can attract abundance by doing good things for yourself, for others, and for God's world. Feed the birds, donate time to your favorite charity, and give those dollars to the musician playing on the street. Perform random acts of kindness for others. It feels good to serve.

Perform these kind actions with an open heart and without expecting something in return. You will not always get the specific item back that you have given out. Yet the universe brings to you a return on your investment. For instance, you might pay for a stranger's dinner; and then you get a phone call from a friend whom you haven't heard from in years. To reap the abundant blessing you deserve in your life, make sure that you *think* and *do* only good to yourself and to others. I know you can do it!

You are invited to continue the relationship at YourAngelChannel.com

Exercise 1: Dream Big

You know you have bold ideas and you've got a lot to give to the world. Start by dreaming big. What would you like to do to give back to the community? Start by asking yourself these questions:

- *What causes do I believe in?*

- *What do I do especially well?*

- *How can I use these unique skills, talents, and abilities of mine to somehow further the causes I'm passionate about?*

- *Out of all the causes I care about, which ONE would I most like to get involved in?*

- *What opportunities exist in my own community to get involved with this cause?*

- *How do I find out about what volunteer opportunities are available?*

- *How much time can I allocate to giving of myself to this cause or charity?*

- *When do I want to start?*

- *How often do I want to do this, at least to begin with?*

You are invited to continue the relationship at YourAngelChannel.com

After you've given the matter careful consideration, make a decision...

I would like to give back by...

_____

_____

_____

_____

_____

_____

_____

_____

_____

_____

_____

_____

Exercise 2: Give It A Try

Now that you've figured out a way to give back by giving of your time, talent, service, and heart, jump in! Give it a try. Find a way to plug into this cause or charity or any type of volunteer work that you desire to be involved with. And make sure to have fun with it.

Exercise 3: Keep A Service Journal

As you begin to volunteer, keep a journal. Describe in detail what service you are performing, and how others are benefiting from this. If someone says thank you, write it down. Whenever you notice that another person has benefited in any way from what you are doing, write it down. Whenever you feel moved by what you're doing, or by someone you've encountered, or by the organization or cause you're involved with, write that down too.

Every so often, go back and read your journal entries. Seeing where you started and how far you've come along will help you see how valuable your service to others really is. Plus, it'll be fun to relive some of those special moments.

Today's Affirmation: It is empowering to give back to others and to the universe. Because I am a dignified, emancipated being, I freely choose to give back. By lending others a helping hand, when I can, I lift them up and I am lifted up. Humanity is about helping one another so that together, my sisters and brothers and I can reach our wonderful shared destiny of abundance.

You are invited to continue the relationship at YourAngelChannel.com

We are on an exciting journey. Abundance is for everyone. When I give, I receive. In giving and in receiving we lift each other up so that all of us can enjoy fabulous riches in our lives. We work together, not against, each other. Instead of competing we cooperate so that everyone can have what she or he needs. What a perfect system! I am thankful and proud to be part of the solution. I make a positive difference.

My Personal Thoughts

You are invited to continue the relationship at YourAngelChannel.com

_____

_____

_____

Today's Action Item

_____

_____

_____

_____

_____

_____

_____

_____

_____

You are invited to continue the relationship at YourAngelChannel.com

---

Think About It

- We are here for each other; when we help another person, we help them reach their abundance, which in turn helps us reach ours. We're in this together.

- When you give back, do so with a thankful heart and a cheerful disposition.

- You have so much to give others. Don't try to solve every problem or meet every need out there—just plug in somewhere that you feel is right for you. With each person doing her and his part to give back, we collectively create joy and abundance for everyone.

You are invited to continue the relationship at YourAngelChannel.com

Conclusion

Your Abundance Outlook

Once upon a time, there was a little girl. She was very special, and she was loved. God gave her unique gifts and sent her on her way so that she could learn, discover, grow, and experience.

As the little girl grew, she brought great joy to others. She trusted the people she loved, and she enjoyed all the delights Mother Earth had to offer—sunshine and rain, flowers and animal friends, long summer days playing outdoors, winter days enjoying the warmth indoors, swimming at the beach, hiking mountain trails, sledding down snowy hills, marveling at rainbows, gazing at the stars at night.

As she gazed at those bright stars stretching across the immense sky, she knew that she was important. She was part of a vast and beautiful creation, so big and so marvelous nobody can quite wrap their mind around it. And she was thankful.

Today that little girl with wonder in her eyes is a beautiful woman, a creation of God, a person of substance, a dear and precious being who spreads light and love wherever she goes. Like the little girl, the woman is special, precious, and unique. That woman is *you*.

Always remember, you are precious in every way! You are worthy, and capable, and absolutely amazing. You are deserving of abundance in every sense of the word. Abundant love. Abundant joy. Abundant wealth. Abundant riches. Abundant relationships.

And please don't confuse "abundant" with "many." This is not a contest. It's not about amassing as much money or collecting as many things or friends as you can. It's about living your life richly, with dignity, grace, strength, and purpose. It's about *quality* of life.

The Meaning Of Abundance

This is one of my favorite dictionary definitions of abundance:

Abundance: *fullness to overflowing*

Doesn't this definition bring to you beautiful images? I envision bright, colorful flowers cascading down a hanging planter. Crystal clear waters bubbling from a spring. An ocean teaming with beautiful aquatic life of all shapes, sizes, and colors. A lush tropical forest, brilliant green and alive, home to beautiful animals on the ground and in the air.

What do you envision? Write it down:

When I hear the phrase "fullness to overflowing," which means abundance, this is what I envision:

You are invited to continue the relationship at YourAngelChannel.com

_____

_____

_____

_____

_____

_____

_____

_____

_____

_____

_____

_____

_____

Make yourself a cup of tea or pour yourself a glass of water, and sit for a moment. As you enjoy your drink, immerse yourself in these beautiful images of "fullness to overflowing." This is what abundance means to you. This is how it *feels* for you.

You are invited to continue the relationship at YourAngelChannel.com

So you see, abundance is not elusive. It's not "out there." It's right here, with you, in your heart and in your soul. You can tap into it anytime, anywhere. It is completely accessible to you. It begins in your heart and in your mind, and it emanates from there. It radiates out of *you*, spreading out to touch every aspect of your life.

Your abundance begins *within*, and it moves outward, propelling you to create opportunities that will bring greater abundance into all areas of your life. You have the power to create "fullness to overflowing" in your sphere of reality!

Bring It On!

Now that you know the secret to abundance in your life, it's time. Bring it on! Keep thinking your way to riches. Give it time—everything worthwhile in life takes a little time. Remember that it's a process, not an overnight event. Let the process unfold like a beautiful flower opening to the radiant sunlight. Keep your focus on your strengths, your gifts, the tasks and activities that will continue to create abundance in your life. Keep moving forward with persistence.

And maintain a thankful outlook. You can turn many of your perceived negatives into opportunities to be grateful …

… next-door kids too loud? Give thanks that you can *hear* them! Give thanks for the new life they represent. Give thanks for children's games and laughter filling the air instead of police sirens and angry shouts. Give thanks.

You are invited to continue the relationship at YourAngelChannel.com

… you became momentarily distracted and burned your dinner? Give thanks that that's all you burned! Give thanks that your angels were watching over you and kept you safe. Give thanks for your home, your possessions, and your food. Open a can of soup, and don't worry about your burnt dinner.

… traffic made you late for work? Be thankful that you arrived safe and sound. Give thanks for your job, for the work that you do. Give thanks for the people around you. Be thankful that you are putting your skills and talents to wonderful use.

… had a disagreement with a loved one? Cool down your emotions and give thanks for your loved one. It's not worth fighting over differences of opinion. Agree to disagree, and then focus on what you love about this person. Give thanks for *all* the special people in your life.

For every negative you experience or perceive, you have the power to turn it around within your own outlook. You can change it from a negative to a positive, just by finding something for which to give genuine, heartfelt thanks. Find the abundance, and be grateful for it.

Bring on your abundance! Let it pour out of you and radiate out to everyone you meet. Let it come back to you many times over. Accept the gifts the universe brings to you. Create, believe, and trust. It's *your* life. Make it an abundant one.

You are invited to continue the relationship at YourAngelChannel.com

Carrie Carter
"The Angel Lady"

C arrie Carter channels messages from the angels and loved ones on the other side.

She has helped thousands of people learn how to use their intuitive abilities to manifest their greatest desires. She is a gifted channel and medium. She channels loved ones in spirit, angels and guides for her clients.

At the age of five, Carrie became aware of her intense abilities of clairvoyance, empathy, and healing. These gifts have given her an amazing ability to empower others to heal from their grief, as she channels messages from their deceased loved ones, angels and guides.

Carrie's passion through her channeling is to help clients connect with God's love to assist them on their journey of peace and happiness in this lifetime.

Angel Vision invites you to experience Carrie's educational seminars, workshops, and personal and confidential channeled spiritual readings and complete life coaching.

She has made numerous appearances on ABC channel 7. She has been interviewed on Fox News Channel 12 about psychics. She was featured in a special program about psychic mediums on ABC Channel 7 News. She has been interviewed on Drive Time talk show Houston News Radio FM 97.5. She was interviewed with BBC radio network in London, and with CBS network radio in Washington DC.

She has been published in numerous news articles which include the LA Times, San Antonio Express-News, Denver Post, and Woman's World magazine. She is noted as one of the ten most expensive psychics in the world.

You can contact here for keynoting, speaking, training, or spiritual consultations at:

+1 – 810-334-7468

www.YourAngelChannel.com

AbundanaireGoddess@gmail.com

➲ **Contact Carrie Carter** about keynoting, speaking, training, or spiritual consultations

Made in the USA
Middletown, DE
23 November 2018